HAVOC for the Holidays

23 heartwarming and heartbreaking holiday plays for grownups

Copyright © 2019 by American Playwrights Press

All rights reserved. This book or any portion thereof may not be reproduced or used in any manner whatsoever without the express written permission of the publisher except for the use of brief quotations in a book review.
Printed in the United States of America.

First Printing, 2019

ISBN 978-1-69-742603-8

Cover photograph by Jon Schulte/Shutterstock.com
Cover design by Kitt Lavoie

American Playwrights Press
Radio City Station
P.O. Box 1973
New York, NY 10101

For Plume and Dovey

Table of Contents

Introduction viii

Snow Ball
by Jennifer Reichert 2
   In junior high, if you don't go with a boyfriend, you're nobody.
   3F; comedy

Empty Handed
by Katelin Wilcox 12
   A bittersweet reunion, and the perfectly wrong gift.
   1F, 1M; drama

Black Sleigh Down, or White Christmas in Machu Picchu
by Jim Fagan 20
   What do you get for the girl who has killed everything?
   1F, 1M; comedy

And it came to pass in those days...
by Kitt Lavoie 28
   A mother-to-be with no place to go, goes to the only place
   she can think of on Christmas Eve.
   1F, 1M; drama

The Seven Men of Hanukkah
by Sharon E. Cooper 32
   A man has the worst audition for the best role ever.
   1F, 1M; comedy

Repeat, Repeat
by Jerzy Gwiazdowski 41
   Maureen's worst student gives her the gift she didn't know
   she needed.
   1F, 1M; comedy

Anyway
by Jennifer Curfman 48
   After the hardest year of their lives, a newly separated couple
   fakes their way through the holiday together.
   1F, 1M; drama

Anniephylaxis
by Julia Bilbao 57
Annie was looking forward to her boyfriend's midnight kiss. She just didn't expect to watch it from the other side of the room.
1F, 1M; comedy

Dear Nate
by Ali Keller 65
Who defriends someone by Christmas card?
1F, 1M; drama

Involuntary Counsel
by Annalisa Chamberlin 72
A brother and sister wrap gifts for their family's last Christmas together.
1F, 1M; drama

Ex-Mas
by Katelin Wilcox 80
Feminism, fidelity, and some sexy reindeer lingerie.
2F; comedy

Fine
by Kitt Lavoie 88
An out-of-work couple confronts the sparse pile of gifts under the tree this year.
1F, 1M; drama

On the Edge of What Might Happen
by Sydney Painter 95
Andy and Ben debate who gets to go first for the biggest moment of their lives.
2M; comedy

Effigy
by Jennifer Reichert 102
On a peak in the Andes, a pair of hook-up buddies see the year out with a bang.
1F, 1M; drama

Year After Year
by Mélisa Breiner-Sanders 112
    One couple... and a Christmas dinner table set for three.
1F, 1M; drama

Believin'
by Sharon E. Cooper 119
    Rothchild is three sheets to the wind. Raymond is in the bag. Literally.
2F, 1M; comedy

IRL
by Will Clark 129
    A man delivers a gift to the best friend he never met.
1F, 1M; drama

Isle of View
by Jerzy Gwiazdowski 136
    An old man surprises his wife with a gift she could never imagine.
1F, 1M; drama

Christmas for New Year's
by Jennifer Reichert 143
    When a medical resident is forced to choose holiday coverage, his best friend hops the first train out of town.
1F, 1M; comedy

Winter Break
by Kitt Lavoie 149
    What do you get for the boy who gave up everything?
1F, 1M; drama

Counting the Days
by Cavan Hallman 156
    An interrogator gives his detainee the gift of baseball for Christmas.
2M; drama

Little One
by Julia Bilbao   164
    A man comes home to his girlfriend and a strange new
    addition to their Christmas tree.
    1F, 1M; drama

Hot Air
by Katelin Wilcox   171
    It's not easy being a 34 foot tall inflatable elf.
    3 actors (flexible); comedy

Playwright biographies   179

Index of song and character inspirations from the
Very Short Holiday Play writing assignment   185

Acknowledgements   189

About The CRY HAVOC Company   191

---

a note on casting

The CRY HAVOC Company supports inclusive and non-traditional casting. The gender casting breakdowns included in this collection are for the plays as originally written, but many of the character genders in these plays could be easily changed. Please contact the playwright if you are interested in changing the characters' genders in your production.

Introduction

In 2009, The CRY HAVOC Company, our not-for-profit new play development theater company in New York City, was in the process of raising money to move into a full-time rehearsal studio of our own. That holiday season, in support of that fundraising effort, six of the company's playwrights wrote new plays for what would become the first of the Very Short Holiday Play collections, to be given to donors as a thank you when they contributed to our new studio fund.

In the years since, this Very Short Holiday Play collection has become an annual tradition at CRY HAVOC – and in that time, 47 playwrights have contributed a total of 134 plays to the annual collections.

Each year, the playwrights were given the same assignment. Each play was to...

- Be no longer than five pages.*

- Take place during the holiday season.

- Feature at least one character from another play that was developed with CRY HAVOC.

- Be inspired by a randomly assigned song (with the songs having a different theme each year).**

Though we originally imagined that these plays would be shared simply with our artists and donors as a fun holiday tradition, we have been delighted to find that many of these plays have gone on to be performed the world over (across the United States, Europe, Asia, Africa, and Australia), published in major anthologies, and even made into award-winning short films.

---

* *Plays were five pages or less in the formatting style of the original annual collections. The plays run a little longer in the format of this publication!*

** *Please visit the appendix in the back of this volume to see the characters and assigned songs that inspired each of the plays in the collection.*

In celebration of the Tenth Anniversary of the Very Short Holiday Plays, we are pleased to share some of the best with you. We hope you enjoy reading them and sharing them with the artists and audiences of your community!

Happy holidays from all of us at The CRY HAVOC Company (whatever time of year you are reading this)!

Kitt Lavoie & Katelin Wilcox
Editors

HAVOC for the Holidays

Snow Ball
by Jennifer Reichert

CHARACTERS
DARLA – female, 13, lanky and tearful
TASHA – female, 13, made-up and glowing
MADISON – female, 13, athletic and timid

SETTING
A teenage girl's basement bedroom

For permission to produce this play, please contact the playwright at:
jennifer@jenniferreichert.com

A teenage girl's basement bedroom, walls covered with posters, an aqua iMac on the desk. DARLA, 13, lanky and tearful, stands looking at her reflection in the vanity mirror. She sings dramatically "Foolish Games" by Jewel.

DARLA   These foolish games are tearing me apart,
              And your thoughtless words are breaking my heart
              You're breaking my heart

She admires the tears and continues, smokily accompanying Jewel.

DARLA   *(cont'd)* You're always brilliant in the morning,
              Smoking your cigarettes and talking over coffee–

She raises her arms and slow dances with an imaginary partner, looking up in his eyes.

DARLA   *(cont'd)* Oh Dylan. Yes. You can kiss me.

A knock on the door. Darla slaps the music off, freezing, then brushing away tears. Another knock.

TASHA   *(off-stage)* Darla? It's Tasha.

DARLA   Get in here! Hurry!

The door opens and TASHA, made-up and glowing, clomps downstairs, carrying a garment bag.

TASHA   I got my cousin's dress! It's perfect for you for the Snow Ball.

DARLA   Close the door!

Tasha clomps back up and closes the door.

TASHA   Why?

DARLA   Madison's upstairs.

TASHA   New Madison? Why?

DARLA   Her mom and my mom are in the same prayer group at church so my mom told her to bring her along to the cookie swap so we can hang out.

TASHA   So you're hiding?

DARLA   She's so... she thinks she's hot snot. Let me see it!

Tasha unveils a white tulle sequined cocktail dress. Darla holds up the dress to herself.

TASHA   You will look slammin', chick. Dylan's eyes are going to pop out.

DARLA   He's never going to ask me. He makes me so crazy. I'll never have a boyfriend. There's no good ones left. I'll have to be alone until high school. Are you *sure* he likes me?

TASHA   Yes. Jeff said, that he said, that you were bangin'. We'll make him ask you and then we can all go together.

A knock on the door. Darla freezes.

MADISON   *(off-stage)* Hello?

Tasha looks at Darla.

TASHA   She knows you're here. C'mon. She's not stuck up, she's just quiet. *(shouting)* Come in!

The door opens and MADISON, athletic and timid, tiptoes downstairs, carrying a plate of cookies.

MADISON   Hi Tasha! Hi Darla. Your mom told me to bring these cookies for us to eat now.

Madison offers Darla the cookie plate. Darla motions for her to set it on the desk. She does.

TASHA That reminds me! Look what I snagged on the way in! Eggnog!

Tasha pulls a carton of eggnog out of her bag and holds it aloft.

DARLA Is there alcohol in that?

TASHA It's eggnog isn't it?

She opens the carton, takes a swig, and hands it to Darla.

TASHA *(cont'd)* Have some.

Darla swigs the eggnog.

TASHA *(cont'd)* Did you find your red scarf for the Christmas Choir Concert?

DARLA Yep.

TASHA Do you have one, Madison?

MADISON I told you guys the concert is the same day as my track meet.

DARLA Hmmm.

Darla takes another swig and catches sight of herself holding the dress in the mirror. She takes another swig and admires the dress.

MADISON Is that for the concert?

DARLA *(disdainfully)* No. It's for the Snow Ball.

MADISON It's so fancy. I don't have anything like that. Just Sunday dresses.

TASHA You should go shopping. Soon. Usually people get semi-formal dresses at Macy's.

MADISON Are they expensive?

Darla shrugs and swigs the eggnog. Tasha takes the eggnog from Darla.

MADISON *(cont'd)* Does everyone in seventh grade go?

DARLA Everyone in 7th *and* 8th. Did they not have semi-formal dances where you came from?

Tasha takes a swig of the eggnog, then hands it to Madison. She gingerly takes a sip.

MADISON Not in elementary. I guess there's prom for the high schoolers. *(beat)* So the Snow Ball isn't just a couples' dance?

Tasha takes a cookie from the plate, takes the eggnog from Madison, and sprawls on Darla's bed.

DARLA Not technically. I mean, last year, all of us popular girls went to dances together, but in junior high, if you don't go with a boyfriend, you're nobody. It's like you didn't even go. If I don't get asked, I'll die. I won't sit with the loser girl group while you and Jeff and everyone are all...

Darla makes handsy slow dancing motions. Madison reaches for a cookie.

TASHA Don't eat the peanut butter kiss, that's Darla's favorite.

Madison takes a different cookie and looks for somewhere to sit.

MADISON Didn't Christopher ask you?

DARLA He's too short. I'd look like his babysitter. Not cute. *(to Tasha)* You better be right about Dylan. It's getting too late for him to ask me.

MADISON Dylan Marlow? The eighth grader?

TASHA	He had to re-take science. They're lab partners.
DARLA	Do you think he asked Becky?
TASHA	No. Everyone would know if Dylan had a date. He's into you. He's just being a boy.

Madison sits in the desk chair.

MADISON	Are you guys a couple?
TASHA	Not yet. But last week he loaned her his jacket on the bus.
DARLA	But he also called me "beanpole" at choir practice. What do I do?
TASHA	Nothing. It's gonna happen, trust me, and then you'll be eating lunch with the 8th graders and forget all about me.
DARLA	I would never. If I'm sitting at the 8th grade table, you are too.
MADISON	He's cool, right?
DARLA	Too cool.

Darla sprawls on her bed and takes the eggnog and swigs it. Tasha shakes her head at Darla and turns to Madison.

TASHA	*(to Madison)* You're going, right?
MADISON	I don't know. I have to talk to my mom.
DARLA	I could tell my mom to talk to her. Everybody goes.
MADISON	I think she will let me, it's just before she said I couldn't date 'til I was fifteen.

TASHA	Date? Who's your date?
MADISON	No one yet.
TASHA	Oh. *(condescendingly)* I'm sure someone will ask you. It's not 'til Friday.
DARLA	*(wrinkling her nose)* Yeah, you have that "new girl" smell. It's fine if *you* go alone, though.
MADISON	I maybe got asked.
TASHA	Really?! Who was it?

Tasha pats the bed between her and Darla.

MADISON	I don't want to say. I don't want to embarrass anybody.
DARLA	Bring the cookies.

Madison brings the cookies and sits between the other girls on the bed.

TASHA	Marc? Chris?
DARLA	Seventh grade boys are so immature.
MADISON	Oh, no. It wasn't–
TASHA	One of those eighth grade hormone factories asked you!
MADISON	Well... yeah.
TASHA	Don't hold out on us, chick.
MADISON	He might have been kidding.
DARLA	Oh c'mon. No one asked her.

MADISON I did get asked.

DARLA Was it Howard? He's so gross. It's alright, he asks everyone. You guys would be a good couple.

MADISON It was Dylan.

TASHA He did not.

DARLA When? He would have said.

MADISON Yesterday. I caught him smoking behind the gym during track practice.

TASHA What happened? What did he say?

MADISON I said he shouldn't be smoking and he said he couldn't help it. So I stole his cigarettes and he tried to get them back, so I put them in my shirt. He said that wasn't fair. I said it was for his own good. And then he smiled and said, "Go to the Snow Ball with me." I said I wasn't sure if I was going, but I'd let him know on Monday.

Tasha sighs and fake collapses. Darla gives her side eye.

DARLA No way that happened. You're just saying that because you know I like him.

MADISON Why would I do that? I'm not a liar.

DARLA How would we know?

Madison scoots off the bed and grabs her purse off the chair. She digs in it and pulls out a half empty carton of cigarettes.

MADISON See?

DARLA Let me see that.

Madison hands her the carton. Darla carefully opens it and pulls out a lighter. Tasha reaches over and takes a cigarette, putting it in her mouth. Darla puts one in her mouth, too.

DARLA (cont'd) Do you think he had these in his mouth?

MADISON Not those ones.

TASHA "Go to the Snow Ball with me, baby."

DARLA You have to say no.

TASHA Yeah, you should go with Marc. He's cute.

MADISON He is. But you said he was immature. Dylan always asks me about my running.

DARLA I liked Dylan first. I've known him longer.

TASHA Marc's a good kid. And she liked Dylan first. It's the friend rule. You can't go out with a guy your friend likes.

MADISON We're friends?

TASHA Of course.

Tasha hands Madison the eggnog. Madison takes a swig. Darla pats the bed next to her.

DARLA Tasha can loan you a dress. Her cousins have tons, if you want to borrow.

TASHA Yeah, I loan them to all my friends.

Madison sits on the edge of the bed. She reaches over and picks up the cigarette carton.

MADISON I think you only want to be my friend because of the friend rule.

TASHA No. We like you. You're cool. We're cool. Don't you want to be friends with us?

Madison slings her purse over her shoulder, takes the lighter back from Darla, stands up and heads for the door.

MADISON I'm gonna go.

TASHA C'mon Madison. You can have the other peanut butter kiss.

DARLA You don't have other girlfriends, Madison.

TASHA Darla! Madison, don't go.

Madison stops and turns back. Tasha pats the bed invitingly. Madison looks at Darla.

MADISON Not here maybe. Maybe here I'll just have boyfriends.

Madison clomps up the stairs and leaves.

END OF PLAY.

Empty Handed
by Katelin Wilcox

CHARACTERS
CLARA – female, 20s/30s, a bright, ambitious woman who recently moved across the country for her dream job

JOSEPH – male, 20s/30s, her long-distance boyfriend, sort of a slacker/late bloomer but he's got a good heart

SETTING
Clara's Chicago apartment, a few days before Christmas

For permission to produce this play, please contact the playwright at:
katelinwilcox@hotmail.com

Lights rise on a small but comfortable studio apartment. Sound of the door being unlocked and a woman talking on her cell phone. CLARA enters, barely visible under heavy winter outerwear, dusted with snow. She hastily removes layer after layer as she speaks into her phone.

CLARA I'm so sorry babe. The driver dropped you off where?? Just tell – tell me what cross streets you're at. *(beat)* Ok great, you're actually almost here. It's the next corner, building number 107. *(beat)* And then buzz 4A. *(beat)* Ok see you soon, love you!

Clara hangs up the call and tosses her phone on the counter. She takes a small drugstore plastic bag out of her purse and pulls out an opened pregnancy test box.

She removes a wad of toilet paper from the box and unrolls it to reveal a used test stick.

She smiles for a moment, then snaps into action, racing to a closet and pulling out a roll of wrapping paper. She rips off a large piece, folds it around the test stick way too many times, sticks a bow on top to secure it, then places it under a tiny Christmas tree on the coffee table.

Suddenly the buzzer rings. She pushes the button.

CLARA *(cont'd)* Come on up!

She scurries around the apartment to clean up, pausing to smooth down her hair and put on some lipstick in the mirror. After a moment, there is a knock at the door. Clara unlocks it and swings it open to reveal JOSEPH, wearing a backpack and a thin winter coat, with what appear to be icicles in his beard.

JOSEPH Chicago. Is. Freaking. COLD.

CLARA *(running to him)* You look like the abominable snow man!

She gives him a big hug and kiss. She starts brushing the snow off him as he awkwardly enters, trying not to track too much slush into the apartment.

CLARA *(cont'd)* I'm so sorry the cab driver got lost, they usually know this area pretty well.

JOSEPH It's fine.

CLARA Well, you're here now. Sit down, let's get you warmed up.

Joseph takes off his backpack and Clara leads him to the couch.

CLARA *(cont'd, teasing)* Honey, you know I love you, but it's really time you got some actual, grown-up-person luggage.

JOSEPH Sometimes it's easier to travel light.

CLARA So. What do you want to do while you're here? Chicago has so much fun stuff going on for the holidays. I can't wait to show you around the city.

JOSEPH Actually, I was kind of hoping we could keep it low key this weekend.

CLARA Oh. *(beat)* Ok. Sure. You know what – I'd be happy if we just ordered pizza and watched Christmas movies the whole time.

Clara snuggles up closer to Joseph.

CLARA *(cont'd)* Or we could just focus on keeping warm all weekend...

Clara starts kissing Joseph playfully. He gently breaks away and clears his throat.

JOSEPH Hey, could I get something to drink?

CLARA Oh sure, sorry.

Clara jumps up and crosses to the fridge, grabbing a bottle of beer.

CLARA   *(cont'd)* I meant to stop on my way home and get that IPA you really like, but I got totally wrapped up in this project we're trying to finish at work – it's amazing how the hours fly by when you actually *like* your job.

Clara hops back on the couch and hands Joseph the bottle of beer.

JOSEPH   This is fine.

He takes a long drink and puts the bottle on the coffee table, where he notices the tiny Christmas tree and the present underneath it. He stiffens.

JOSEPH   *(cont'd)* What's that?

CLARA   ...A surprise.

A beat.

JOSEPH   Clara, we said we weren't doing gifts this year.

CLARA   I know, but–

JOSEPH   I didn't get you anything.

CLARA   You're my Christmas present.

Clara kisses Joseph again, this time more intensely. Joseph breaks away forcefully.

CLARA   *(cont'd)* What's wrong?

Joseph takes a deep breath and faces Clara.

JOSEPH   Clara, this isn't working.

CLARA   What?

JOSEPH   Us. This. It isn't working.

CLARA   Whoa. Okay, slow down. Joseph – we knew long distance would be hard. But it's just temporary.

JOSEPH   No it isn't.

CLARA   I know it feels that way now. We haven't seen each other in two months, and I've missed you too–

JOSEPH   It's not that–

CLARA   –but you're the one who made this arbitrary rule that we should wait till I got settled before you moved here – well, I'm settled! Move here. Move to Chicago.

JOSEPH   I don't want to move to Chicago.

A beat.

CLARA   Ever?

JOSEPH   No.

A beat.

CLARA   Why didn't you tell me that when I got the job? This is my dream job, Joseph. I can't just get a job like this anywhere.

JOSEPH   That's why I didn't tell you. I figured I'd wait it out, see how it went. Maybe you wouldn't like it. Maybe you'd come back. But I didn't want you staying just for me.

CLARA   I wouldn't have. *(beat)* Joseph – I don't get it. I know it's cold, and the football team sucks, but what's really so bad about Chicago?

JOSEPH   I know you don't get it. It's just... not home.

CLARA Then what's so great about home?! You're a bartender, who spends every Monday night watching football with his dad, and whose best friend is his ten year old nephew.

JOSEPH You don't understand. You're not close with... Family's not important to you. If you make me choose between my family and you, you will lose. Everytime.

CLARA Well I'm sorry but, it's not as simple as "them or me." Things get complicated when there's an "us." It's time to grow up and face that, Joseph. *(beat, collecting herself)* Look, I think we're both maybe getting caught up in the heat of the moment. Let's just take a breath. Why don't we sit down. You should open your present.

JOSEPH What? Clara. I just told you I think we should break up.

Clara picks up the present and holds it out to him.

CLARA Joseph, I know you better than you think I do.

JOSEPH What does that mean?

CLARA Just open the present.

JOSEPH Clara, I feel bad enough as it is.

CLARA Ok then shouldn't you at least just do what I'm asking you to?

Joseph takes the present and slowly begins to unwrap it.

CLARA *(cont'd)* I know how much family means to you. And I know that one day, there's gonna be a little kid who thinks you're the best dad in the world.

JOSEPH Clara, I would love that, but the real problem is – I've never pictured you as the mom.

Clara freezes for a moment, then snatches the present out of Joseph's hands just before he gets it unwrapped.

JOSEPH *(cont'd)* I thought you wanted me to–

CLARA What did you just say?

JOSEPH Look, I think a part of me knew we weren't right for each other, and once you were gone, it just confirmed it.

CLARA So... it's not that you don't want to move to Chicago. It's that you don't want to move to Chicago for me.

JOSEPH Clara you're right. It's time for me to grow up. And when I think about my future – you're just not "mother of my child" material.

A beat.

CLARA Is that why you came? To tell me this?

JOSEPH I thought I should do it in person.

CLARA *(realizing)* Sometimes it's easier to travel light.

JOSEPH I changed my ticket. I'm going back tonight.

CLARA Well thanks for stopping by. You better run along back to Mommy and Daddy before anything gets too hard.

JOSEPH Come on, Clara. Do you think this was easy? This *is* me growing up. Wouldn't it have been easier for me to just do this over the phone? But the ticket was

JOSEPH *(cont'd)* booked and I thought, you know what – make the tough choice. You owe her that.

CLARA Merry Christmas to me.

Joseph grabs his backpack and crosses to the door.

JOSEPH I'm sorry, Clara. *(beat)* I hope...

CLARA What??

JOSEPH I... hope you didn't spend too much on the Christmas present.

A beat.

CLARA It's fine. I can return it.

Joseph exits. Clara stares after him for a moment, then looks down at the present in her hands. Lights down.

END OF PLAY.

Black Sleigh Down, or White Christmas in Machu Picchu

by Jim Fagan

CHARACTERS

LEAH – female, a superspy, American, currently a "freelancer" and not above a dirty contract if it suits her moral compass. A fighter/runner/gunner, depending on need. She is at the top of her game.

PETER – male, an ok spy. Good at disguise. Great at lying. British. He is at the medium of his game.

SETTING

Machu Picchu, Peru, South America
December 24
23:50:00 (PET)

For permission to produce this play, please contact the playwright at:
JF3.Creative@gmail.com

(13.07° S, 72.35° W)
A Valley Near Machu Picchu, Peru, South America
December 24
23:50:00 (PET)

Sound of a helicopter getting closer. LEAH sprints and dives into a clearing and settles on the edge of a MOSS-COVERED ROCK. From her pouch she quickly pulls a blanket of moss-like material— throwing it over herself seconds before a large helicopter searchlight passes over her.

Stillness as the sound recedes. She pulls off the moss, opens her pack, and cocks her Glock 26 pistol, strapping it to her ankle. Then, she assembles a M82a1 / M107 Barrett Sniper Rifle, slings it over her shoulder, checks the scope, and fixes it on the distance. She swaps it with a pair of night vision goggles, checks her target, then, sighing, still not satisfied, removes a candy cane from a small breast pocket and chews on it unceremoniously.

Helicopter sounds. She drops her candy cane in the dirt. The chopper doesn't get close. This ticks Leah off. She slings a long tube off her back and effortlessly pieces together her M3 Carl Gustav Rocket Launcher. She lays a missile next to it, eyeing the sky as if to say, "Just try it."

Suddenly, she freezes. No breathing, no blinking, just listens. Then, in one fluid movement she whips her GLOCK out and aims it, locked and steadied, at the moss-covered rock.

LEAH   Out.

A very proper British voice responds from the MOSS.

MOSS   I see they gave you the full set of kitchen cutlery for Christmas.

LEAH   OUT.

MOSS   If you're going to crash my spot, I'd appreciate it if you didn't alert the entirety of the Shining Path to our presence.

Leah cocks her weapon. PETER pulls off his own moss-like blanket. He wears a full tuxedo.

PETER (cont'd) Nice to see you again, Agent.

LEAH (*holstering her gun*) You've got to be kidding me. (*beat*) Agent.

PETER You look fetching as always.

LEAH We can't all look like James Bond.

PETER (*looking at himself*) Right. Tonight was a black tie affair hosted by the public front of the Shining Path Party. I thought I'd have a night cap by paying their private backers a visit. Pure intel. And you? Starting an all out drug war or are we just blowing up Machu Picchu?

LEAH Classified.

PETER Really. An actual assassination? Who's pissed off America this week?

Leah gives him a look that says, "If I told you, I'd love to kill you," and goes back to scoping out the territory below. Peter settles in close, but not too close.

PETER (cont'd) So what are we doing here? Smoke them out? Classic rocket launcher into the mess hall? He comes running out into the open and in the confusion you give him the old "King and Country," or whatever you call it... "Presidential Mandate?" You know if you end up setting fire to that compound you risk making half of South America high as a kite.

LEAH If you're going to be here, shut up.

PETER Well well well well now. We're allies. Last I checked.

Silence.

PETER *(cont'd)* Is this about Kathmandu? Because really...

LEAH I am here working. If you continue to act like an obstruction I will treat you like one and *remove* you.

This has some effect. A helicopter sound, but far off. Leah loads the rocket launcher.

PETER What do we think? Security, or trafficking?

She glares at him.

PETER *(cont'd)* Well reasoned.

The two sit in silence. Leah is fixed on her target. Peter is fixed on her.

PETER *(cont'd)* So you're proper freelance now. Word gets around. I'm here with NATO, actually. I'm a genuine peacekeeper so let's keep it peaceful huh?

Almost imperceptible, Leah scoops a handful of dirt.

PETER *(cont'd)* So... After the quick strike, then what? Hop the border? Hide out? Since you're on your own and all, if you need a place to sta–

Leah throws the dirt in Peter's eyes.

PETER *(cont'd)* Ahhhh!

She swiftly kicks Peter directly to the chest, but he's ready for the next blow. They exchange a volley of punches, kicks, parry and counters—

LEAH Stay the night? As if I'd–

She punches him rather than finish her thought.

PETER I only meant to say if you were freelance then that meant you took the Assignment on your own free will... Gah woman, my eyes!...

He lands a punch.

PETER *(cont'd)* It would mean you're all alone tonight of all nights and that would mean...

Leah lands an impressive kick to the throat, which shuts Peter up for the moment. He staggers to the ground. She whips out her signature WICKED SAW TOOTH BLADES. Everyone in the espionage world knows her by these blades. You rarely see these and live to describe them.

PETER *(cont'd, struggling with his throat)* Abou... ughhh... Just... glahhh... Kath... man... du.

LEAH *(pressing the flat end of the blade to him)* Just listen. I took this job for one very specific reason. One. Because I wanted to be alone tonight and this seemed to pretty much guarantee it. ALONE. That's first. Second, I did my homework. This area is an operative dead zone. NO NATO ACTIVITY Sanctioned. Completely, utterly, alone. Guaranteed. So, I'm going to ask you just one time, and if you lie, I'll kill you. And I'll *know* if you're *lying*. What are you doing here?

PETER I came for you.

LEAH Well, you failed.

She lifts the blade above her head ready to drive it home.

PETER No, not like that... bugger. Wait! I'm Martin Keene!

LEAH Martin Keene's an old man. He...

PETER He hired you. Which is to say, I hired you. Since I'm him. Well, I'm not actually him, as you know, I'm

PETER	*(cont'd)* British Secret Service. Well, former, now, really. Defector. You know... "Off with his head!" and all that. That's news to you. I've assumed the identity of Keene. To, um, reach... to hire you. To get you here.
LEAH	Say more...
PETER	I wanted to... Jesus this is embarrassing... I wanted to run into you. Again. Like Kahtmandu, that night. That night was so... and you are so... I even dressed up for the occasion.
LEAH	Oh my god. This mission is made up.
PETER	Sort of. Not really, I did *actually* hire you.
LEAH	I was going to assassinate Yatala!
PETER	Well... He's not a good guy anyway...
LEAH	Are you out of your mind? I could have been killed! I could have–
PETER	Please. You must understand. I've wanted... I've thought about you... and, after that night, I couldn't stop. Like you said, you said that night when we were... Which was incredible, by the way. Night of my life, really... But then you said how it can be so lonely... Which I never thought of before, so thanks a lot for that because after that I started crying in the middle of missions, totally unprovoked, until it really started screwing up my work. Fact is, everywhere I went on mission I just wanted to run into you. And I started to dream – we just run away together, screw the mission, you know – to Kathmandu – It got so... Well, I had to get out. See, I'd worked up a lot of money over the years, bit off the top, you know – and I quit. But then, I was *still* lonely, and... and the problem, turns out, wasn't the work at all, it

PETER	*(cont'd)* was me. More specifically, me *without* you. See? So, I heard you went freelance from a buddy of mine at The Company. And I just had to see you. Only, you're not the kind of girl one just looks up. So I made this plan... I thought, just maybe, you're freelance now, you could get out, I'm defector, we're both free. Don't you see? Oh, and I *borrowed* this tux and I hadn't even thought about James Bond I swear.
LEAH	Lonely? I said that? Out loud?
PETER	Dawn glistening off your back. It was just about my favorite moment ever.

They stare at each other in silence. Helicopter sounds go unheeded. The spotlight from the Helicopter settles on them. It's romantic, until it starts shooting. Leah shoves Peter, hits the ground, rolls to her launcher, and fires it up into the sky. It connects. We hear a massive explosion. Big globes of white come floating down from the sky.

PETER	*(cont'd)* Huh. Festive.
LEAH	I think this is coke.
PETER	Could be, could be. *(beat)* Happy Christmas.
LEAH	Yeah, Merry Merry. *(she's going to say... but then...)* We should run.
PETER	Opposite directions.
LEAH	Probably. *(beat)* Peter, that night. For me. Um... too. *(beat)* But don't you ever pull this again, or next time I *will* kill you!
PETER	Will there be a next time?

She aims her sniper at him, its neat, red laser dot settling on his forehead. He freezes. She approaches him carefully, lowers the gun, and kisses him.

LEAH Next time, *I'll* find you.

They sprint off in opposite directions as we hear dogs barking and soldiers shouting.

END OF PLAY.

And it came to pass in those days...
by Kitt Lavoie

CHARACTERS
TED – male, restless soul in his mid-20s
CASSIE – female, a pretty if decidedly unexceptional girl in her early 20s

SETTING
Ted's apartment – an unimpressive box of a one bedroom in a small American city

For permission to produce this play, please contact the playwright at:
kitt@kittlavoie.com

Lights rise on Ted's apartment — an unimpressive box of a one bedroom in a small American city. TED, a restless soul in his mid-20s, sits in his grease-stained work shirt, his snow-caked boots and socks strewn around his feet, mindlessly sipping a mug of hot chocolate while watching "Rudolph the Red Nosed Reindeer" on TV, an open and half-eaten blue tin of Danish cookies in front of him on the coffee table. On the wall hangs a lone stocking. A scrubby, foot-tall evergreen festooned with too many Christmas lights sits on the endtable next to him.

A knock on the door.

Slightly puzzled, Ted goes to the door. He opens it, revealing CASSIE, a pretty if decidedly unexceptional girl in her early 20s. It's hard to tell if the redness of her cheeks is from tears or the wind or both. Ted could not be more surprised to see her.

TED Cassie.

CASSIE Ted.

A long, uncomfortable pause. Ted looks at her. Cassie can't quite look at him. Finally...

CASSIE *(cont'd)* I'm sorry. I shouldn't have—

TED No. Come in. Please.

Ted steps out of the doorway. Cassie steps inside. Ted scampers to the couch, muting the television and stuffing his wet socks inside his boots, then placing them neatly under the coffee table. Behind him, Cassie removes her snow-topped hat, unwinds her long scarf, and unzips her heavy coat — revealing a large pregnant belly. She slides out of her coat as Ted turns around, seeing her unzipped for the first time. He stops cold. He looks from her belly up to Cassie's eyes. She gives him an awkward, shrugging grin.

TED *(cont'd)* Can I get you...? I have cocoa. Or, here— *(offering the tin of cookies)*. They have the little pretzel kind. I know you—

CASSIE I'm alright. Thanks.

They look at each other in the glow of the television, Cassie hovering by the door. Ted gestures for Cassie to sit. She makes her way to the couch and sits. He sits next to her on the far end of the two-seat sofa. A long moment. Then...

TED How's Mark?

CASSIE Gone.

TED Where?

CASSIE I don't know. "West" he said.

TED There's a lot of west.

CASSIE Yeah. We went to the doctor. He took one look at the sonogram and said, "That doesn't look a goddamned thing like me, Cass. How do I even know it's mine?" Right there in front of the technician he said that. And then he dropped me off. And wished me a Merry Christmas. And a Happy New Year. And he left.

TED Maybe he's coming back.

CASSIE I don't think so.

Cassie reaches into her pocket and pulls out a neatly creased sheet of paper. She offers it out to Ted. He unfolds the sonogram.

CASSIE *(cont'd, with a smile she can't suppress)* It's a girl.

Cassie's smile melts away to tears. She turns and studiedly watches the muted television. Ted studies the sonogram. Then Cassie. A long silence. Then...

TED Is it—?

CASSIE It's his, Ted.

TED Okay.

Ted turns to the television. The silence of the room is heavy as they both watch the flickering light of the television for a long, long time.

CASSIE   I'm sorry, I shouldn't have come here...

Cassie hastily rises and shambles her way towards her snowy coat.

CASSIE   *(cont'd)* I just didn't know where else to go.

She grabs her scarf and begins winding it around her neck.

TED   Wait.

CASSIE   No, I should go.

TED   Sit. I have something for you. A present.

Ted heads into his bedroom. Cassie stays where she is. Ted can be heard rummaging in the other room. He emerges with a small box wrapped in colorful but well-worn balloon wrapping paper. He offers it out to her.

CASSIE   How did you know—?

TED   It was for your birthday. Before...

Cassie looks at him a moment, then turns her attention to the box. She tears away the paper and opens the box. She looks inside, then up at Ted.

TED   *(cont'd)* You can always come here.

Ted takes a breath and walks to the couch. He sits, watching the silent television. Cassie reaches into the little box and lifts out a key.

She looks at Ted a moment, then walks around the couch, unwinding her scarf as she does. She sits next to him. He picks up the remote from the cushion next to them and un-mutes the television. The sounds of Rudolph, Santa, and Burl Ives fill the silence between them. Cassie lays her head on Ted's shoulder — and they watch together as the lights fade to black.

END OF PLAY.

The Seven Men of Hanukkah
by Sharon E. Cooper

CHARACTERS
STEPHANIE MULLINS – female, 30s, has a secret
PHIL – male, 30s, an actor, has had a recent loss

SETTING
A room in a community center, the present

For permission to produce this play, please contact the playwright at:
www.sharonecooper.com or secooper1@yahoo.com

STEPHANIE, 30s, wearing a suit and heels, sits behind a desk. There is a banner behind her that reads: "Welcome to the Audition!" There is a knock at the door. Stephanie adjusts her glasses, takes a deep breath and writes on a pad of paper.

STEPHANIE Do come in.

A man who used to be good looking but is looking a little haggard, PHIL, 30s, enters. Stephanie finishes writing. Stands. Smiles. Phil smiles. They stand and smile.

STEPHANIE *(cont'd)* I'm so glad you could make the audition.

PHIL I am too. Well–

STEPHANIE Well–

PHIL I brought a headshot.

He hands it to her.

STEPHANIE *(reading)* Nice, nice. I see here that you went to school.

PHIL Um, yes, yes I did.

STEPHANIE *(reading)* Special skills: juggling, driving, stage combat – that must help you develop your biceps, right?

She smiles at him.

PHIL Uh, sure.

She takes off her glasses.

STEPHANIE So, why don't you tell me a bit about your *acting*.

PHIL I'm classically trained but mostly enjoy working on new plays. Where you get to be in the room and see

PHIL   *(cont'd)* the play evolve. Be a part of something from the very beginning.

STEPHANIE   I feel the same way.

PHIL   So, this is – great. Just great.

STEPHANIE   Yes.

PHIL   *The Seven Men of Hanukkah*. That's a great title. Great title.

STEPHANIE   Thank you. One man for each night. *(passing a piece of paper to him)* And here are your sides for Man Number Three.

PHIL   *(overlapping)* Huh – then why seven men? Hanukkah lasts for eight nights.

STEPHANIE   Well, everyone knows *that*. That would be the obvious choice. To have eight men for eight nights, but instead, there will be seventeen because that's a big enough group for a real fight scene, you know?

PHIL   But the play is called *The Seven Men of Hanukkah*.

STEPHANIE   So, yes, wonderful, just go ahead and read.

PHIL   *(reading)* "I love *you* like I have never loved another Stephanie. *You* are the one for me. *You, you,* YOU Stephanie." I'm sorry, your name is –

STEPHANIE   St–rawf–anie.

PHIL   St–rawf–anie. And what exactly is this play about?

STEPHANIE   It's kind of a mash up really of play ideas – in a play. It takes place with *men* during Hanukkah, fighting, around a Christmas tree. And there's a love interest,

STEPHANIE *(cont'd)* named Stephanie, and also Noah's ark and the splitting of the Red Sea.

PHIL Right, so, could you explain how—

STEPHANIE We will talk about all of that when we are in the rehearsal process! You have been offered the role of Man Number Three. Shalom!

PHIL Um—, thank you. Shalom means hello — or goodbye — or peace.

STEPHANIE Exactly. So hello and peace to this project until it's goodbye. If you could just give me all of your contact info—

PHIL I, um, generally like to read the script before I commit to—

STEPHANIE Oh, I can't provide it just *now* — I thought you liked to see a play evolve.

PHIL Plays are generally written *before* auditions.

STEPHANIE Of course — the play — is written.

PHIL The sides you gave me were two lines.

STEPHANIE As a professional thesbian—

PHIL So, I'm sorry, I think I'm unavailable.

Phil begins gathering his coat.

PHIL *(cont'd)* So good luck with—... whatever—... and happy—... whatever—

He's walking out the door.

PHIL *(cont'd)* And it's thes*pian,* not *thesbian.*

STEPHANIE Wait. Stop. I– I'm only auditioning *you*.

He stops. Turns. Returns.

PHIL Why? And why would Sam say I had to do this? How do you even know–

STEPHANIE Through Sam's dog walker, Jody, who knows my cousin–

PHIL I haven't gotten a part in months and this is the part he said I *had to come out for* – *the part that was written just for me?*

STEPHANIE Well, it was kind of written just for you.

PHIL Oh my God.

STEPHANIE I didn't want to meet you, you know, so awkwardly, like over coffee.

PHIL *(to Stephanie)* Yeah, this was much less awkward. *(getting it)* OOhhhhh. This. This thing is like a set-up? For a date. A date.

STEPHANIE I would call it a first *meeting* – of friends of ours who think we might want to meet. So, a meeting. Sort of. Of new people. Together. Meeting. For the first time.

PHIL But instead of just *meeting* in, say, a bar–

STEPHANIE Raymond and I don't drink.

PHIL Who's Raymond?

STEPHANIE My– cat. He only drinks water – out of a fountain – it kind of makes me want to pee all the time.

PHIL   Couldn't you all have come up with a better play or lines or a *plan*–

STEPHANIE   I know, it was just, this might surprise you, but I'm not a playwright.

PHIL   Really? This is the best play–

STEPHANIE   It's not the *best* play–

PHIL   No, no it's not! I don't know what you, Sam, Jody or your cousin the dog walker were thinking–

STEPHANIE   *(overlapping)* The dog walker is not my cousin – my cousin is–

PHIL   Whatever!

STEPHANIE   *(overlapping)* I'm just so tired of getting to know someone, sitting across from men in cafes, drinking stale tea, asking *What do you do? What do I do?* My life is a series of getting to know yous instead of being already known, you know? And what I know about you is that you haven't had a good audition since she died. And I thought I could give you one.

PHIL   Is there anything you don't know about me?

STEPHANIE   Lots.

PHIL   Funny, I don't know anything about you.

STEPHANIE   Well, I um, eh, er, I've watched every episode of *Friends*.

PHIL   Great. That's just wonderful.

STEPHANIE   And these glasses aren't real. I just wanted to look sexy. And smart. Like a librarian. Like a sexy, smart librarian.

PHIL   What do you *do*?

STEPHANIE   I'm a vet.

PHIL   Really?

STEPHANIE   Well, I play with the animals. Volunteer. It's not exactly the same. I–I'm kind of between things right now. But I do love animals. Like I'd generally rather be with them more than people.

PHIL   Me, too.

STEPHANIE   I would be so heartbroken if anything happened to Raymond. I've had him for fifteen years. How old was she?

PHIL   Nineteen. Phyllis had this beautiful double coat and was tan with black saddle. I kind of feel like, what good am I without her?

STEPHANIE   How are you coping?

PHIL   I run around the dog park with her friends. It's not the same.

STEPHANIE   Of course it's not.

PHIL   And the holidays are the worst.

STEPHANIE   My holidays were the worst. At Christmas, my parents would scrape together whatever was left after they paid Con Ed and bought us socks and sweaters, and we'd go to New York and wait in line, in the cold, for half price tickets. My fingers would still be cold when we sat in the theatre – but when the lights went up, it was like anything was possible. It was fun and exciting and playful and more joyful than life. And I just want meeting people to be–

STEPHANIE   *(cont'd)* fun. And joyful. Like when did we stop having fun? And why?

PHIL   I'm not Jewish.

STEPHANIE   Yes you are. Sam says you like bagels – and Sam's Jewish.

PHIL   Well, I'm not.

STEPHANIE   Oh.

A moment. She turns away. He starts scribbling on a piece of paper. She continues.

STEPHANIE   *(cont'd)* You know, the period between Thanksgiving and New Year's is like an endless night. It actually starts closer to October. Around Halloween when it's okay to be someone you're not. I usually play a witch and Raymond plays my cat.

He laughs. She notices him writing on the sides he auditioned with earlier.

STEPHANIE   *(cont'd)* What are you doing?

PHIL   Audition.

He hands her a piece of paper. She reads.

STEPHANIE   "I love *you* like I have never loved another. *You* are the one for me. *You, you,* YOU Strawfeny." It's St–rawf–anie. My name is St–rawf–anie. I'm sorry. I'm sorry I wasted your time.

PHIL   Keep reading.

STEPHANIE   *(reading)* "Act One, Scene One. A man and a woman in an empty room. The woman is acting like a crazy turd and the man is rather handsome, gorgeous actually. He hasn't auditioned for anything in a long

STEPHANIE *(cont'd)* time. Until today. Apparently, neither has she. There's something really endearing about — him. And she's not so bad, either. Lights up."

Blackout.

END OF PLAY.

Repeat, Repeat
by Jerzy Gwiazdowski

CHARACTERS
MAUREEN – female, 31, an English teacher
GUS – male, 10, a fifth-grade student

SETTING
A fifth-grade English classroom. December, 1985.

For permission to produce this play, please contact the playwright at:
jerzygwiazdowski@cryhavoccompany.org

A fifth-grade English classroom. December 1985. Handmade Christmas decorations adorn the walls, though they are in the process of being un-decked: garland half-dangling, piles of discarded snowflakes and stars pulled from the wall, and a garbage can in the center of the room.

MAUREEN, 31, enters, on the phone, carrying the receiver into the room, cord dangling behind her. She gets it as far inside as she can and continues cleaning up her classroom, taking down handmade Christmas decorations from the walls and placing them in the trash.

MAUREEN   I don't know, Craig. What do you want me to say?

Maureen pulls a Santa off a nearby wall and crumples it.

MAUREEN   *(cont'd)* Well, I'm not going to say that.

She tosses the Santa-ball into the bin from a distance.

MAUREEN   *(cont'd)* Because I'm not sorry. I said what I meant. I don't want to go this year. And she doesn't want me.

The phone cord is taut. Maureen places the receiver on her desk and stretches to pull decorations down from the far wall. She grabs a cheery-looking snowman from the wall.

MAUREEN   *(cont'd)* She'll only be disappointed if you're not there. It's a family holiday, and "I'm not part of the family," remember?

Maureen tosses the snowman into the trash, then pulls a red and green felt stocking from her purse.

MAUREEN   *(cont'd)* Well, it's her house. And her fake tree. And her slimy ham.

Maureen picks up a lumpy construction paper snowman. She stops. She pulls the cheery snowman from the trash and examines the two side by side.

MAUREEN   *(cont'd)* Well, then you can eat it. Eat it! I can make do with peppermint schnapps, ugly snowmen, and gifts from my students.

Maureen looks into the stocking. She turns it upside-down. Several lumps of coal tumble onto her desk.

MAUREEN   *(cont'd, re: the coal)* Oh, come on. *(into phone)* I don't get to have Christmas this year, Craig. I'm on the bad list.

Maureen looks at the lumpy snowman. GUS HERBRECHTSMEIER, 10, enters. He's red-cheeked, backpacked, tracking snow through the door. One of those kids whose mouth is always hanging open. Maureen does not see him.

MAUREEN   *(cont'd)* I'm not trying to be difficult. I AM difficult. So just go without me.

She hangs up.

MAUREEN   *(cont'd)* Gack.

She takes the lumpy snowman and rips it into dozens of confetti pieces, sprinkling them into the trash, whistling the tune of "Let it Snow."

GUS   Hey, Miss Dugdale?

She turns to see Gus.

MAUREEN   Mother— *(she catches herself)* Hey, Gus. Where's your mother?

GUS   In the car. We kinda turned around.

MAUREEN   Oh. Gotcha. Did you forget your house keys again?

GUS   No.

MAUREEN   Backpack?

GUS No. I told her I had to go pee.

MAUREEN You told her you had to go "to the *restroom*." Well, then you should probably go.

Gus just stands there.

MAUREEN It's Christmas break, Gus— you don't need a hall pass.

GUS I don't actually have to pee— Sorry— I don't actually have to …rest.

MAUREEN Then why did you tell your mother that?

GUS Because I was lying.

MAUREEN I got that. Why?

GUS Because I don't want her to know why I really came back.

MAUREEN And why is that?

GUS I came back to get my snowman.

MAUREEN Your snowman.

GUS Yeah.

A beat.

GUS *(cont'd)* Did you just throw it away?

MAUREEN Yes.

GUS Why?

MAUREEN You know Gus, I could report you to the honor committee for cheating.

GUS What?

MAUREEN Copying another student's work is very serious. It's unethical. Even on a snowman.

GUS Oh.

MAUREEN One of these days, Connor isn't going to be next to you to copy from. Or, he won't let you anymore. And frankly, I don't know why you're cheating off of *Connor* anyway. You shouldn't cheat off *anybody* BUT– You'd get better grades if you cheated off Andrea Bonkowski.

GUS Andrea doesn't like me.

MAUREEN Maybe she's *difficult*.

GUS No, it's because I put peanut butter in her hair. But Connor doesn't care if I cheat off of him.

MAUREEN That doesn't make it right.

GUS I know – I feel really bad. He lets me do whatever I want. He asked if he could make a snow fort with me and my brothers and I told him I couldn't because I'm grounded. But I'm not grounded. Then he asked if I wanted to make a snowman, and I said that my family didn't believe in snowmen. But we do believe in snowmen. Then he made that one in class, and he wrote me a note saying "to my friend Gus Herbrechtsmeier. We can make a snowman together." But I'm not his friend. I just copy off him.

MAUREEN Gack.

GUS He even spelled my last name perfect.

MAUREEN "Perfectly."

GUS You can't even spell my name most of the time, Miss Dugdale. But Connor is always doing really nice stuff for me and all I do is make fun of him.

MAUREEN I'm sorry, Gus. The snowman is gone.

GUS This is going to ruin my whole Christmas.

MAUREEN Well, I hope you learn your—

Maureen stops mid-sentence and heads to her desk.

GUS Learn my what?

Maureen pulls the stocking from her desk and places the coal lumps in.

MAUREEN Take this.

GUS Why are you giving me coal?

MAUREEN It's for Connor. It's his present, from you.

GUS But coal is for bad kids.

MAUREEN That's not coal.

GUS Yeah it is.

MAUREEN It's a snowman.

Gus looks at her, mouth agape.

MAUREEN *(cont'd)* Just add snow. Take that to Connor's house and show him that you care.

GUS Thanks, Ms. Dugdale.

MAUREEN Now go before your mom gets worried. See you next year, Gus.

Gus looks at her again, quizzically.

MAUREEN *(sighs)* I'll see you in three weeks. Have a good break.

GUS You too, Miss Dugdale.

Gus exits. Maureen continues to pull down decorations. She stops, picks up the phone and dials.

MAUREEN *(cont'd)* Hey – listen. I changed my mind. No, no- I'm not going there, not a chance. But I do want to have Christmas this year. With you. I don't care what we do. We can build a snowman or something. But your mom is right. It's a family holiday. And you are my family.

Blackout.

END OF PLAY.

Anyway
by Jennifer Curfman

CHARACTERS
EMILY – female, 33
BENNETT – male, 35

SETTING
A half-packed living room

For permission to produce this play, please contact the playwright at:
jencurfman@gmail.com

Lights rise on a small living room. Large cardboard packing boxes are stacked around the room and some scattered furniture holds its own among the boxes. A basket of wrapped Christmas gifts sits on one of the boxes. EMILY, 33, enters from the kitchen with a wrapped platter of cookies and a shiny holiday gift bag, which she adds to the basket. She glances out the window and gazes down to the street below. She sighs and leans against the window ledge as she unbuttons her coat.

There is a knock at the door. Emily walks to the door, takes a breath, and swings it open. BENNETT, 35, steps through the door into the entryway. He is wearing a wool coat, and he carries a bottle of wine.

BENNETT Hi Em. I'm sorry. I had to—

EMILY Yeah. Well, I sent the car away. We're already late. We have to wait for another one. Come on in.

BENNETT Yeah.

Bennett enters the living room. He stands aside a bit awkwardly and takes in what he sees.

BENNETT *(cont'd)* Jeez. You've made a lot of progress in here.

EMILY My sister flew in last week to help.

BENNETT Carrie? She's in town?

EMILY Yeah. I close on the new place next month. *(pointing to a pile of boxes)* Those three are yours. And you still have a few things in the hall closet too.

BENNETT Okay. I'll make a plan to get them when I get back after New Year's.

EMILY You're going to...? Okay.

BENNETT How is your sister?

EMILY She was fine. Good, even.

They look at each other for a moment and he raises an eyebrow at her. She smiles, just a little.

EMILY *(cont'd)* Okay, it was kind of nuts. But. I needed the help. And the wine. She'll be there later today. I'm pretty sure she's going to behave herself.

BENNETT Oh, great. We'll see.

EMILY Give her a break. She promised to try. This is hard for everybody.

BENNETT It's been hard for me too.

EMILY I'm sure.

She takes a breath.

EMILY *(cont'd)* I'm sorry. I know that. I do.

Bennett checks his watch and glances out the window. They are both quiet. For a while.

BENNETT How are you feeling lately?

EMILY Can we not?

He is quiet. A beat. She checks her phone.

EMILY *(cont'd)* Six minutes away.

BENNETT Okay.

Bennett leans against the window ledge. They are quiet again, for a moment.

EMILY You and... you guys are going away for New Year's?

BENNETT ...Yeah. We're... we're going to the cabin with the guys.

EMILY Oh. Cool.

She tries to smile. A beat.

BENNETT Come on, Em. What the hell are we doing? Small talk? Why do you even want me here today?

EMILY I absolutely don't. This is for my dad. He asked you to do this. I told you that, Bennett.

BENNETT Jesus, Emily. I don't know what to say to you. Yes. We have plans for New Year's. I'm trying like hell to make a life. I've apologized to you every way I know how. I'm here today and I don't even understand why. I'm trying.

EMILY No. *I'm* trying. I'm trying to be okay. I'm trying not to be mad. But it doesn't go away just because you're sorry. I have to make a new life too.

BENNETT Look, Em. I thought I could do this for you today. I really tried to be okay with this insane plan so we could celebrate your remission with your family. But I thought that you wanted me there. I don't think I can go with you if the only reason I'm there is to pretend we're together so your grandmother doesn't freak out. Practically everybody else knows. This is ridiculous. I have apologized to you a thousand times. You know that. But I don't owe you this Christmas charade.

EMILY But you're so damn good at charades.

BENNETT That's not fair.

EMILY Damn it, Bennett. This barely scratches the surface. *We* were supposed to have plans. *We* are supposed to be making a life. Do you have any idea what this New Year's is supposed to mean to me? What this stupid Christmas means to my family? This is supposed to be a *better* Christmas. A *good* Christmas. Do you even remember last year?

BENNETT	Don't you dare. Of course I do. *Why do you think I'm here?*
EMILY	You sat with me in the hospital *on Christmas* and looked me in the eye and told me how I would be okay and you let me tell you all those stories about what we would do this Christmas. You promised me that "next year will be better." And you knew the whole time that you were leaving me.
BENNETT	You asked me to make you that promise. And I wanted it to be true. And yeah, I waited, Em. *Of course* I waited to tell you. What else was I supposed to do?
EMILY	You know what? Fine. You don't owe me anything. You owe it to my dad. You promised him you would be here for me. In sickness *and in health*. They trusted you. They thought I was in good hands with you.
BENNETT	You were.
EMILY	I thought I was.
BENNETT	Are you kidding me? You were. This doesn't cancel everything we had, everything we've been through.
EMILY	Don't be naïve, Bennett, it really might. My dad can't look my grandmother in the eye and tell her that, oh, never mind, you won't stick around to take care of me after all. I sure as hell can't ask him to look her in the eye and tell her that you decided to spend Christmas with your boyfriend instead of your wife.
BENNETT	Em. I am here because I love you so much that I will keep pretending today just because you asked me to. I did give up Christmas with Jarvis. For you. I am here even though you don't actually want me

BENNETT *(cont'd)* here. I will obviously do anything for you. That hasn't changed. You know that, Emily. But I cannot owe you forever.

EMILY Congratulations. You're the big, brave hero, stuck here on Christmas, pretending that you actually love me.

BENNETT But that's *exactly* what you're asking me to do.

EMILY They are throwing a special Christmas. Just for me. And if I have to suck it up and go pretend I'm glad to be there, then you have to come pretend too. My grandmother has no idea about us. That's why my dad wants you there. She thinks this is just a celebration. That I'm out of the woods and you and I are going to live a long happily-ever-after. And that's never going to be true.

BENNETT I can't change that. And you're never gonna forgive me for it, are you?

EMILY I told you I'm trying. And I do know you're sorry. But I'm not even allowed to be mad at you because you're just being who you are. You're the brave one for coming out and I'm just supposed to be fine and happy for you. Humiliated and abandoned, but totally fine.

BENNETT I did not abandon you.

EMILY Are you kidding me? Just because you didn't run to Jarvis while I was still sick?

BENNETT This isn't just about you, Em. Of course you get to be mad at me. But not forever. And not today.

A beat.

BENNETT *(cont'd)* Well, this was a great idea. A real pleasure. Merry Christmas. I'm gonna go.

EMILY Fine. Go. Thanks.

Bennett starts to move toward the door. He stops and turns back to her.

BENNETT No, you know what? You owe me too. I know this sucks for you, but you blew it. You were supposed to be my best friend. We were a team. You were supposed to understand.

EMILY I know I was. We *were* a team. You should have told me. A really long time ago.

BENNETT Maybe you should have known.

EMILY Exactly. You made a fool of me. For years. And now I get to be a fool for Christmas.

Bennett chuckles a little.

EMILY *(cont'd)* Shut up.

BENNETT Sorry.

EMILY I'm serious. This isn't funny to me. You should have trusted me. Way before I got sick.

He takes a breath.

BENNETT Em. No one thinks you're a fool.

She gives him a look.

BENNETT *(cont'd)* Really. And I really am sorry I couldn't tell you before.

EMILY I know you are, Bennett. But I'm still so angry at you and I feel stupid and embarrassed and scared

EMILY *(cont'd)* and... just mad. But. I know you're sorry. I just don't know what to do with that yet.

BENNETT ...Yeah. I know.

She looks down at her phone.

EMILY The car's here. I'm gonna go.

BENNETT I'm gonna come with you.

EMILY No, you were right. This was insane. I won't ask you to keep hiding. I'll go handle my family. You should go to... to Jarvis.

BENNETT Nah. He's with his brother. Trust me, I'd rather face your dad.

Emily stands and starts to button her coat.

EMILY I don't know what I would have done without you last year. It's still hard to figure out what I'm gonna do now.

BENNETT Me too. You know that, right?

EMILY Yeah.

BENNETT How 'bout, as a start, we go see your family for this celebration? It's a pretty good cause. And I did promise that we would have a better Christmas this year.

EMILY I don't know. Last year might be hard to beat.

BENNETT We can talk to your grandmother. Together.

EMILY That feels like a terrible plan. And not exactly the "better" Christmas the rest of them are dreaming of.

Bennett smiles.

BENNETT I think they'll be okay. Especially since you are.

EMILY Maybe.

BENNETT And you can be mad at me all day if you want. It'll be fun.

Emily smiles a little.

BENNETT But Em, pretty much everybody in your family already knows. I don't want to pretend with them anymore.

EMILY I know.

Emily picks up the basket of gifts. She gives Bennett a long look and hands him the basket. She opens the door and turns back to pick up the cookie tray. She looks back at Bennett.

EMILY *(cont'd)* Okay. Let's go.

BENNETT Yeah.

She heads out the door. Bennett takes a deep breath. He takes a quick look around the living room, picks up the bottle of wine, and heads out the door, pulling it shut behind him.

END OF PLAY.

Anniephylaxis
by Julia Bilbao

CHARACTERS
ANNIE – female, 26 years old
TREVOR – male, 26 years old

SETTING
A fancy hotel room, New Year's Day, approximately 12:07am

For permission to produce this play, please contact the playwright at:
julbilbao@gmail.com

Lights up on the bedroom of a hotel suite in a five star hotel.

ANNIE, 26, storms in wearing a silver gown. She kicks her heels off and throws her clutch onto the bed. Hastily grabbing a number of belongings, she begins packing a small suitcase.

TREVOR, 26, rushes in wearing a dapper tux and smoothing out his disheveled hair.

TREVOR Annie. Slow down...

Annie ignores him and marches into the bathroom.

TREVOR (cont'd) Annie. Wait.

ANNIE Happy New Year, Trevor! HAPPY NEW YEAR. Happy HAPPY <u>HAPPY</u> NEW YEAR TO YOU. I hope it's EVERYTHING you wanted it to be.

TREVOR Stop packing. Can we talk about this like adults?

Annie re-enters with an armful of makeup, hair styling tools, etc.

ANNIE Oh, you want me to handle this more maturely? Handle something my boyfriend just did that was so embarrassingly "high school" more maturely? What the hell was that?

TREVOR I have no idea – she jumped me! She made out with my face. There was no time for me to even think about what was happening before it was over!

ANNIE Really. You didn't have any time to think? You weren't thinking, "hmm, why am I pouring my *ex-girlfriend* a glass of champagne as everyone is counting down to the New Year? Hmm... where is my current girlfriend so I can give *her* a glass of champagne? I'd really love to kiss *her* on the New Year. God, she really looks beautiful tonight. She really–"

TREVOR I'm not the one who was ignoring my boyfriend all night getting my father's rich friends to give money to my precious Kickstarter!

ANNIE I'm not going to apologize for being ambitious. You know these millionaires are most generous when they're liquored up.

TREVOR Yeah, well, it's New Year's. There's a time and place for that.

ANNIE There's no time or place for cheating on your girlfriend right in front of her face!

TREVOR I didn't cheat on you! I was ASSAULTED.

ANNIE And don't you dare accuse me of neglecting you. I'm not the one who was downstairs at the casino all last night with Luke doing God knows what.

TREVOR I invited you! You suggested we go to Staples to buy a paper shredder so I can throw my money away more productively.

ANNIE And I stand by that! You can't do casinos, Trevor. Especially based on what happened last time.

TREVOR You *know* that guy at the blackjack table was spooking the dealer!

ANNIE That doesn't mean you punch him and break his nose! I can't call my father again to bail you out of jail. Next time that happens, you're on your own — You're changing the subject.

TREVOR You started it.

ANNIE UGH. I *hate* you! And Leila is still in love with you.

TREVOR Do you blame her?

ANNIE   Oh my god... I've never found you more attractive.

Annie resumes packing her suitcase.

TREVOR   Annie. I love you. Okay?

Ding ding. Trevor's phone goes off. He pulls it out of his pocket and quickly sends a text.

ANNIE   Who was that?

TREVOR   Luke. Just wondering where we went.

Trevor cautiously moves towards her. He puts his hands on her hips and pulls her closer to him.

TREVOR   (cont'd, in his best George Bailey voice from It's A Wonderful Life) What is it you want, Annie? What do you want? You want the moon? Just say the word and I'll throw a lasso around it and pull it down. Hey. That's a pretty good–

ANNIE   That does *not* work for everything, Trevor... Maybe cut the George Bailey impression and start with wiping her coral pink lipstick off your neck.

Annie pushes him away as he frantically wipes at his neck. She slumps down on the edge of the bed.

TREVOR   I'm sorry, Annie. If it makes you feel any better she was eating the lobster. Her kiss could've killed me.

ANNIE   Where *is* your Epi pen?

TREVOR   It's... it's in my pocket.

ANNIE   Show me.

Trevor awkwardly fishes through his pockets.

ANNIE	*(cont'd)* You can't, can you? Because as usual, you forgot it. And I've been a good little girlfriend carrying it around in my tiny clutch all night just in case my poor little boyfriend's throat closed up. I sacrificed my lip gloss to fit that thing in here!

She snatches her clutch off the bed and chucks the pen at him. Trevor shoves the pen into his pocket when ding ding! Another text. Trevor quickly turns his phone on silent.

ANNIE	*(cont'd)* It's her isn't it?
TREVOR	Annie. No.
ANNIE	Then show me!
TREVOR	No!
ANNIE	Why not?
TREVOR	Why can't you just trust me? You won't even tell me your passcode.
ANNIE	It's 8738! Show me!

She dives at him trying to wrestle the phone out of his hand. He pushes her back onto the bed.

TREVOR	Annie, cut it out! You're acting crazy.
ANNIE	I need this to have never happened.
TREVOR	Well it did. And I hate it too.
ANNIE	Do you? Do you hate having two beautiful women wanting you for themselves?
TREVOR	I thought she was beautiful until I met you! There's no comparison, Annie. I only want you, okay?

ANNIE You looked pretty happy with her.

TREVOR I was being *nice*. She was smashed and talking about how lonely she was. How I took all our friends after the break-up. I felt bad.

ANNIE I'm glad you have feelings, Trevor. But I'd like you to have them for me. To want to spend time with me. But instead you're avoiding me all the time like I'm a cater waiter serving shrimp cocktail.

TREVOR I do *not* avoid you.

ANNIE You want to know the real reason why I was talking to my father's friends all night? Because you were talking to her all night. I know you haven't seen her in a while. I don't need you to stop talking to her. But you *kissed* her. I saw the whole thing. Yes, she was wasted and all over you... but you pulled her in too. And the fact that you're denying it hurts the most.

TREVOR I was trying to keep her from falling over–

ANNIE I am so sick of excuses, Trevor. If you want to be with me then *act like it*.

TREVOR 3... 2... 1...

Trevor swiftly pulls Annie from the bed and into a passionate kiss.

TREVOR (cont'd) This year will be different, Annie. I promise. But I need you to trust me.

Annie kisses Trevor this time and they find themselves in a warm embrace.

ANNIE I'll try.

TREVOR You'll see. I won't let you down.

They resume kissing and it quickly becomes more heated. Their hands start to wander. Annie removes Trevor's jacket and begins unbuckling his belt. She unzips her dress as Trevor kicks of his pants leaving them in a bundle on the floor. Annie playfully pushes him onto the bed and grabs her clutch. She looks through it.

ANNIE Guess I also couldn't fit a condom in here...

TREVOR *(gestures at floor)* Pants pocket in my wallet! I'll be right back, I gotta pee.

Trevor jumps up and runs to the bathroom.

ANNIE You always forget your Epi pen but god forbid you forget condoms.

Annie picks Trevor's pants up off the floor and fishes through his pockets. As she's pulling out his wallet something else falls to the floor.

It's a poker chip and on one side is a coral pink lipstick kiss mark.

Annie's face drops. She looks over her shoulder at the bathroom and back at the poker chip.

She reaches back into his pockets and pulls out his phone. She stares at it for a moment and calmly puts it back as Trevor exits the bathroom, jumping back on the bed.

TREVOR Alright. Where were we?

Annie moves slowly. She straddles Trevor on the bed and gently kisses him on the cheek.

ANNIE The worst part is that I still love you.

Suddenly, Trevor erupts in a pained howl, gasping for air. Annie gets up off of Trevor revealing an Epi pen in his thigh. Trevor yanks it out and sits up, gasping for air.

ANNIE (cont'd) You should probably have a passcode too. Leila's "ready for you upstairs." She can't wait to "pick up where you guys left off last night."

TREVOR (effortfully) I'm– sorry–

Annie retrieves her shoes, throws on her coat and grabs her suitcase.

ANNIE Hope you can breathe easy this year, Trevor.

Annie flicks the poker chip from her hand onto the bed next to Trevor. She exits leaving him alone in the room.

END OF PLAY.

Dear Nate
by Ali Keller

CHARACTERS
NATE – male, 33
CHARLIE – female, 20s

SETTING
Outside a modest home on Long Island

For permission to produce this play, please contact the playwright at:
alikeller@cryhavoccompany.org

NATE, 33, is sitting in the snow holding a Christmas card outside a modest home on Long Island. He is wearing an ugly Christmas sweater and a Santa hat with the name "Cookie" written across the white part in glitter puffy paint. CHARLIE, a female in her 20s, also wearing an ugly Christmas sweater walks outside and plops down next to Nate. They make an odd, but complementary pair.

NATE   We're at a party.

CHARLIE   Actually we're outside a party.

NATE   You should be inside. You wouldn't want our colleagues to think we're friends.

CHARLIE   I'll go back when I know you're okay.

NATE   Because you care so much.

CHARLIE   So much.

NATE   If that's true, then you really suck at making cards.

CHARLIE   I thought it was pretty clear.

NATE   Nothing says you care like *(reading from the card)* "Dear Nate, I'm friend dumping you – Merry Christmas."

CHARLIE   I guess it's really more direct than clear.

NATE   Why are you out here?

CHARLIE   Because when a grown man walks away from the drunk co-worker dressed like slutty Mrs. Claus who's throwing herself at him to sit in the snow, alone, somebody should make sure he's okay.

NATE   I'm fine. You can go back to your *friends* now.

CHARLIE   Don't be so dramatic.

NATE Dramatic? You could have told me you were mad at me last night at the bar, or last week at the movies, or at any day at work, but you decided to end our friendship with a construction paper Christmas card you gave me during a party I'm hosting. I can't even leave. Why didn't you just tell me?

CHARLIE I wanted to be the one to end our friendship.

NATE When did we decide it was ending?

CHARLIE When you couldn't bring yourself to hold my hand.

Nate looks at her like he doesn't know what she's talking about.

CHARLIE (cont'd) On the LIRR. *(beat)* After I put my head on your shoulder, you got so tense I thought you stopped breathing. *(beat)* Then you went to hold my hand and changed your mind.

NATE I just didn't want you to read anything into it. You've been so moody lately.

CHARLIE I've been moody because you refuse to be alone with me anymore at the bar or the movies. For the past two weeks the only time we've been alone it's been at morning update meetings and even then you keep the door open.

NATE I never refused to be alone with you – it's not like you've asked for one-on-one time.

CHARLIE You said, "we both need to work on controlling ourselves," which meant I need to work on controlling myself.

NATE I said "we."

CHARLIE But you meant me.

NATE You don't know that for sure. You're only twenty-four, you don't know everything.

CHARLIE I know how old I am.

NATE Do you? When I was twenty-four–

CHARLIE Yes, I know, you were twenty-four before I was, congratulations. Pointing that out all the time is really annoying.

NATE You don't get to end our friendship because you're annoyed at yourself for not being able to handle a few drunken mistakes.

CHARLIE You may be older, but you don't know everything either, like maybe using the word mistake might not be the best choice ever. And having sex five times, which is more than a few, is not why our friendship is ending.

NATE Well nothing else has changed–

CHARLIE I changed.

NATE You said you could handle casual sex.

CHARLIE I can, but I didn't realize that's not what this was for me.

NATE You should have told me you had feelings before we slept together the first time.

CHARLIE I didn't know.

NATE How could you not know? It's not like the sex was so good it changed your mind.

CHARLIE Oh I know. If it was, we'd be having a different conversation right now.

NATE You don't know that.

CHARLIE Maybe you don't.

NATE Because you know me so well.

CHARLIE No, because I've seen you have that conversation with people you don't even like.

NATE You haven't been around most of the women I've dated.

CHARLIE It's the only positive thing you say about the women I have been around for. The ones I've watched you convince yourself to keep dating.

NATE It doesn't mean that if our sex was better I'd want to date you.

CHARLIE Sure.

NATE It also doesn't mean we can't be friends.

CHARLIE I know.

NATE Then why is this happening?

CHARLIE I told you, I wanted to be the one to end our friendship.

NATE We just agreed that it doesn't have to end.

CHARLIE It doesn't have to, but it's going to.

NATE What are you even saying right now?

CHARLIE My feelings aren't why this is ending. Bad sex is not why this is ending. This is ending because you suspecting I have feelings for you makes you awful.

CHARLIE	*(cont'd)* It's like you second-guess everything you say or do around me.

NATE	Well now I know—

CHARLIE	The idea that I maybe, might, have feelings for you has made you act like a terrified dog but now that you know for certain that I have feelings for you, it's going to make you totally normal again?

NATE	I'm just trying to make things easier for you.

CHARLIE	I've had my heart broken before, I'll bounce back. It's the lack of faith you have in my ability to do that that hurts.

NATE	Well I'll try to stop doing that, just give me a little time to adjust.

CHARLIE	Every time you tense up to make me feel better, it's a reminder that you're ashamed that we happened and of me.

Nate opens his mouth to respond but stops himself. Charlie waits.

NATE	I won't freeze up again, I promise.

CHARLIE	You can't make a promise like that.

NATE	Let me do something.

CHARLIE	There's nothing to do.

They sit in silence for a moment before Charlie moves to get up.

NATE	So for the past two weeks you've—

CHARLIE	I tried to verbalize it – at the bar, at the movies, hell I even tried at work, but even with all your insane

CHARLIE *(cont'd)* behavior you still look at me the same way. Like you've been waiting for me.

NATE Right.

CHARLIE I'm too twenty-four to stand up against the look.

NATE You're a mature twenty-four.

CHARLIE I ended a friendship via a Christmas card, I'm not that mature.

NATE If you change your mind—

CHARLIE You'll be waiting?

NATE Yea.

Charlie kisses Nate on the forehead and leaves. Nate watches her walk down the street until she's out of view. He waits.

END OF PLAY.

Involuntary Counsel
by Annalisa Chamberlin

CHARACTERS
MAGGIE – female, 17, a senior in high school; normally brilliant and effervescent, emotional exhaustion is beginning to take a toll on her. Tends to take on far too much and often gets taken advantage of by others. She is close to her younger brother, Scott, and is protective of him.

SCOTT – male, 12, a little small for his age, or so he's been told. Works hard to measure up to his older sister, Maggie, who is always there for him and always knows what to do. Likes to fix things and is utterly lost when facing the reality of their parents' problems. A romantic and hopeful soul.

SETTING
A fairly ordinary bedroom filled with the chaos of last minute gift-wrapping and decorating – paper, ribbons, presents, empty tree ornament boxes, etc. Late in the evening on Christmas Eve.

For permission to produce this play, please contact the playwright at:
chamberlinannalisa@gmail.com

A plain bedroom. White walls. The appearance of newness, but almost too clean and new; not quite homey. SCOTT, 12 and small for his age, in a faded pair of flannel pajama pants and a Batman t-shirt, lies on his stomach with his face buried in the pillows. All around him on the bed, floor, and dresser are strewn reams of colorful wrapping paper, bows, ribbons, scissors, tape and a variety of old cardboard boxes. A pile of presents, wrapped meticulously in glittering paper sit against the foot of the bed. Scott lies motionless, except for an occasional shudder. He is trying very hard to stifle his emotions. There is a cautious knock on the door.

MAGGIE   Scottie?

After a heavy silence, MAGGIE, 17 and counting, carefully opens the door and softly steps into the room. She is wearing raspberry pink-striped pajamas underneath an oversized track sweatshirt. Dark circles under her eyes indicate a severe lack of sleep.

MAGGIE   *(cont'd)* Hey, buddy. Can I come in for a couple minutes?

Scott makes no sound. Maggie nods at the pile of presents.

MAGGIE   *(cont'd)* We still need to put those under the tree. Just a few hours left before Christmas...

SCOTT   *(groaning)* Whatever. You're the one who's good at arranging things. Just do it without me, okay?

MAGGIE   But... we always do it together. It won't be the same. I need you to help me decide which ones to hide in the back to save for last.

Scott sits up and looks at her. His face is bright red, his eyes are puffy. He is heartbreaking.

SCOTT   Nothing is ever going to be the same. That's the whole point.

Fresh tears spill down his face and he throws himself back into the pillows in despair.

MAGGIE	Hey... hey... we don't know anything for sure yet... Oh, buddy... oh, please don't cry.

Maggie sits on the edge of the bed and gently shakes his shoulder.

MAGGIE	*(cont'd)* Hey, come on. It's really not the end of the world. We still have this Christmas all together and– Here, roll over and talk to me. Please?

Slowly, he rolls over and stares straight up at the ceiling.

SCOTT	It *is* the end of the world. What are we going to do? Mom and Dad... What are we going to do?!? Oh, my gosh, this is the worst Christmas and the worst year and I don't even know!

MAGGIE	Scottie, we don't know anything for sure yet. They're just talking about it. You know? I mean, it's a pretty big decision. I'm sure they're still going to think a lot about it.

He sits up and looks at her.

SCOTT	Then why did Mom talk to me about it if they're not sure?

MAGGIE	I don't know. I... I think that she probably wants to be honest with us... just in case–

SCOTT	If Mom and Dad get divorced I'll kill myself–

MAGGIE	Scott!... Okay... Woah, seriously, calm down. Don't say that.

SCOTT	I will! We're a family and they're just going to break it all up and I'll be miserable.

MAGGIE	Well, aren't you miserable now? I can't stand being here anymore.

SCOTT	You don't have to be here anymore! I just started junior high and you're graduating high school at the end of the year. What about me? I'm not good at comforting Mom like you are, Dad barely talks to me about anything... You know my friend Jackie?

MAGGIE	That little redhead with the pet iguana? Yeah. I like her.

SCOTT	Her parents got divorced. Now she lives in an apartment with her mom and her mean Aunt Susan. She gets to see her dad for one holiday so every year she has to pick to not have Christmas with one of her parents... Even if you do come home for Christmas it might not even be here! And I don't want to *pick* between Mom or Dad! And after Christmas... I'll just be alone. I'll have to go back to school and everyone will notice when Dad isn't there to pick me up and I have to take the bus instead. I don't know anyone on the bus. *(pauses, weighing his next words)* Can I show you something?

MAGGIE	*(surprised)* Yeah. Sure.

Scott rises from the bed and goes to the dresser. He opens the top drawer and lifts a pile of socks up to retrieve a small white envelope, slightly yellowed around the edges. He returns to the bed and hands it to Maggie.

MAGGIE	*(cont'd)* What... is this?

SCOTT	Look at the date. It was their first wedding anniversary.

Maggie carefully slips a piece of paper out of the already torn end of the envelope. She unfolds the worn paper and begins to read.

MAGGIE	"To my sweetheart"... Oh my gosh... "To my sweetheart: You are so wonderfully sweet, cute, sexy, smart, beautiful, and everything good. You make my whole world perfect. I can't wait to come

MAGGIE	*(cont'd)* home and hold my darling wife at the end of each day. I'm so lucky to be married to you, baby! Happy Anniversary! I love you! Love, your Hunny Bear..."
SCOTT	—I found it when I was bringing up wrapping stuff from the basement. It was stuck to the bottom of a shoebox. *(beat)* We should put this with one of Mom's presents. One of the nice ones.
MAGGIE	Do you think so?
SCOTT	Don't you think it will make her happy to read it again?
MAGGIE	*(carefully)* I... totally see what you're saying... But I'm not sure...
SCOTT	I think it's a great idea.
MAGGIE	No, really. I don't think we should.
SCOTT	Yes we should! It's almost Christmas and we have to do something to–
MAGGIE	Dad's not in love with Mom anymore.
SCOTT	What?
MAGGIE	Things change when you've been with someone for twenty years.
SCOTT	Just shut up, Maggie.
MAGGIE	Dad said it, not me. Every time I try to talk to either of them and see if they're okay they end up venting to me like I'm their therapist or something. Seriously, trust me, I don't think this is a good idea.
SCOTT	Why?

MAGGIE It would be one thing if it really came from Dad, but coming from us it will just remind her that he doesn't do nice things like that anymore. She says he doesn't tell her she's beautiful anymore. Maybe she'll be happy for a second and then Dad will have no idea what's going on and *she'll know* it's not from him and she'll be devastated. On Christmas. No. I don't want to risk it.

SCOTT So we just do nothing? Okay, Maggie, let's not even try! Let's just give up on them!

MAGGIE (*deeply offended*) Oh really? It's my fault now because I don't want Mom to get hurt? They're the ones who are giving up! *I* don't know why! *I* don't have any answers! (*bursting into tears*) They're the ones giving up. He's giving up, she's giving up! AND NOW EVERY NIGHT HE'S SLEEPING UPSTAIRS AND SHE'S CRYING IN MY BEDROOM AT FOUR IN THE MORNING! (*barely able to breathe between sobs*) I can't watch her cry anymore. It's killing me.

SCOTT (*nearly screaming*) Stop screaming! You're being hysterical like Mom.

MAGGIE (*in hysterics*) I'm not being hysterical! I'm s-sad! And – angry! Am I allowed?! God, you sound just like Dad.

SCOTT (*outraged*) I do not! Screw you, Maggie!

MAGGIE *Then don't make me feel stupid for crying and don't try to make it my fault!!!!*

There is a heavy stillness. Maggie struggles to quiet her sobbing and Scott sits in silence. After several deep breaths, she wipes her face and slowly rises to her feet. She walks around the bed and starts to pick up some of the presents from the pile.

MAGGIE (*cont'd*) Let's get the rest of these under the tree before they get back from mass.

Scott doesn't move. She turns and walks to the door. She stops and turns.

MAGGIE *(cont'd)* Scottie... I'm sorry I said that. I... Let's just have Christmas now, okay?

Silence. He lowers his head and wipes his nose with the back of his hand. He looks up at her. She turns to the door.

SCOTT MOM AND DAD ARE GETTING DIVORCED.

Silence. Maggie turns to face Scott.

MAGGIE Yes.

SCOTT I'm not okay with it.

MAGGIE *(at a loss)* Neither am I.

Maggie stands there holding the presents, not sure what to do next.

MAGGIE *(cont'd)* Do you want to help me figure out where to put all these?

SCOTT Yeah. I'll be right there.

Maggie moves for the doorway.

SCOTT *(cont'd)* Maggie?

She turns back again.

MAGGIE What?

SCOTT I love you, sis.

She smiles, a little taken off guard.

MAGGIE I love you too, bro. *(nodding her head to the hallway behind her)* Come on. Only a couple hours until Christmas!

She turns and exits with her armful of presents.

Scott moves to the pile of presents, scoops up an armful, more than he can carry, and a couple boxes slip out of his arms to the floor. He freezes for a moment, staring down at something on the floor. He checks the door. He puts the presents down and picks up the letter from off of the floor, gently smoothing out the paper. Slowly, softly he reads it to himself...

SCOTT   ..."you make my whole world perfect"...

With a resolve beyond his years, Scott sighs, folds the letter, returns it to its envelope, reseals the flap down with a strip of Scotch tape, and tucks it under his pillow. He gathers a smaller armful of presents, pausing for a moment in the doorway, before exiting through the open door. Lights fade to black.

END OF PLAY.

Ex-Mas
by Katelin Wilcox

CHARACTERS
SUSAN – female, 20s, hurt, humiliated, and out for justice
HOLLY – female, 20s, cool and collected

SETTING
A trendy lingerie store, New Year's Eve

*For permission to produce this play, please contact the playwright at:
katelinwilcox@hotmail.com*

Lights up on the interior of a trendy lingerie store. It is New Year's Eve, and the racks and mannequins display "holiday-themed" merchandise for an after-Christmas sale. HOLLY, a young sales associate who is... rather well-endowed... is organizing and straightening items. After a moment, another young woman, SUSAN, enters. She takes a deep breath, then charges up to Holly.

SUSAN Are you proud of yourself?

HOLLY Sorry, what? *(flustered)* Um, can I help you with something?

SUSAN Seriously?

A beat as slowly it dawns on Susan...

SUSAN *(cont'd)* You don't know who I am, do you.

HOLLY ...No. Sorry.

SUSAN God, I didn't think this could get any more humiliating.

Susan starts to exit.

HOLLY *(quickly, relieved)* Okay, well, thanks for stopping in. Have a happy New Year.

Susan stops dead. She turns to Holly.

SUSAN What did you say?

HOLLY Nothing, just "Happy New Year." Bye.

SUSAN You know what, I think I'll take a look around. Since I'm here.

HOLLY Oh. Ok. I'll be over here if you need anything. All the holiday merchandise is 60% off.

Susan starts browsing the racks distractedly, but mostly watching Holly. Holly pretends not to notice.

SUSAN　　Got any big plans for the countdown tonight?

HOLLY　　Not really. Probably do a little party-hopping. You?

SUSAN　　I *had* some plans. But they... fell through.

A beat. Susan holds up some ridiculous get-up, a "sexy reindeer" outfit or something.

SUSAN　　*(cont'd)* Do people actually wear this stuff?

HOLLY　　You'd be surprised.

SUSAN　　*(smugly)* I guess I'm just used to the stuff at *my* store.

HOLLY　　Oh, are you a designer?

SUSAN　　*(deflating a bit)* No, no the... the store where I work. *(recovering)* It's just a little more... classy.

HOLLY　　Where do you work?

SUSAN　　Macy's.

HOLLY　　Oh. Yeah, I guess the crowd we're targeting is a little more... on trend.

A beat.

SUSAN　　And this is the trend?

HOLLY　　For some people.

SUSAN　　*(pointedly)* Would *you* wear it?

HOLLY　　Sure. Why not. It's fun. Look, all this holiday stuff is a little bit of an acquired taste.

SUSAN   It sure is. *Holly*.

Holly looks down at her nametag. A beat. Holly smiles sweetly at Susan.

HOLLY   Yeah. I guess, not everybody can pull it off.

SUSAN   You know what, I think I'll try it on.

HOLLY   Great. What size are you?

SUSAN   *(quietly)* 34B

HOLLY   34D?

SUSAN   No, B – like "boy." *(Susan looks down at her flat chest.)* Like... boy.

A beat. Susan is clearly embarrassed.

HOLLY   I'll go check in the back.

Holly heads for the stock room.

SUSAN   Forget it. I'm not wearing this slutty crap.

Susan slams the sexy reindeer get-up back on the rack.

HOLLY   Whoa – look, no one's forcing you to.

SUSAN   *You* are forcing me to.

HOLLY   Me?

SUSAN   You, and every other woman who *does* agree to wear this stuff, who I have to compete with.

HOLLY   It's not a "competition."

SUSAN   Easy for you to say. You won.

A beat.

HOLLY You know what, I think you should go browse the "unmentionables" counter at Macy's with your Grandma and leave me alone. When I was the first girl in my class to need a bra, no one was handing me a blue ribbon. They were too busy drawing tits on my locker.

SUSAN And now you work here. Where you delude women into spending ridiculous amounts of money in the name of "female empowerment" and "owning your sexuality" when it's really just some desperate attempt to keep a guy interested. Or an excuse to skank it up and steal some unsuspecting chick's boyfriend.

HOLLY Some women *like* putting a little effort into keeping their guy interested.

SUSAN You wanna talk about effort? *(beat)* He was a mess when I met him. And I don't just mean dirty dishes and month-old laundry, I mean *he* was a mess. I took care of him. He cut back on the drinking, and the pot. The sober nights actually started to outnumber the blacked out ones. Hell, he even started eating vegetables once in a while. I took care of him.

HOLLY ...Congratulations.

SUSAN And what do I get for it? The morning I go to pick him up to meet my *parents* at Christmas dinner, he's passed out with lipstick all over his face and a bedazzled thong in his fist.

HOLLY Well maybe he needed to get laid more than he needed a mommy.

SUSAN He needs *me*.

HOLLY   No he doesn't. Look, I'm sorry to break it to you, but when people cheat it means things aren't working. It's an ugly way to say it, but it's pretty damn effective.

SUSAN   So I should just walk away? "Sorry to have wasted your time, I hope you two are very happy together"?

HOLLY   It's better than tracking her down on Facebook and harassing her at her job in the name of feminism.

A beat.

SUSAN   What do you, like, get off on humiliating people or something?

HOLLY   No. You did a pretty good job of that yourself. *I* tried to give you an out. "Thanks for stopping in. Have a happy New Year." You're the one who decided to stick around and be the world's most pathetic ex-girlfriend. I've been dealing with girls like you since the seventh grade. You were jealous, little teenagers who turned into jealous, *(re: Susan's chest) little* adults. I'm so over it.

SUSAN   Oh, really? If you knew who I was then I'm clearly not the only one who did some Facebook stalking.

HOLLY   Please. I saw your picture on his dresser.

SUSAN   GROSS. *(beat)* Wait – you saw my *picture*? Before... or after?

Holly does not respond.

SUSAN   *(cont'd)* So, before. You're unbelievable. You don't even feel bad about it.

HOLLY   What do I have to feel bad about?! *He's* the one who cheated! He's responsible for his own actions. I was just out having fun.

SUSAN   On Christmas Eve. You got drunk and went home with a stranger on Christmas Eve. And *I'm* the pathetic one?

HOLLY   Your boyfriend cheated on you the night before he was supposed to meet your parents. He was not "the one." It's better you find that out now, rather than a year down the road. *(quietly)* Trust me. *(beat)* You said yourself he was a mess. You should be thanking me.

SUSAN   Thank you. So much. For assisting in his epic fall off the wagon. Nobody's heard from him in days. *(beat, quietly)* He might have been a mess, but he was *my* mess. And he was getting better. You know, tonight was going to be the first New Year's Eve in my *life* that I actually had someone to kiss at midnight. Not some desperate rando at a party, but an actual *someone*.

HOLLY   Well, then I guess we'll be in the same boat.

A beat as Susan processes this.

SUSAN   You mean – you haven't heard from him either?

HOLLY   Sorry to bust your Brad and Angelina rage-fantasy, but c'mon. We hooked up at a bar. It wasn't exactly love at first sight. It's not my fault his dumbass friends decided to plaster the photographic evidence all over the internet.

A beat.

SUSAN   You thought you were just soooo irresistible, with your– *(gesturing to Holly's chest)* and– and– your– *(gesturing to the rack of lingerie)*. Well. Look what it got you. You'll be just as pathetic as me tonight.

A beat. Holly takes a deep breath.

HOLLY   Is there anything else I can help you with?

Susan starts to exit. She stops at the door, but doesn't turn around.

SUSAN   Who's going to take care of him?

HOLLY   He can go take care of himself.

A beat. Susan exits without looking back at Holly. Lights fade.

END OF PLAY.

Fine
by Kitt Lavoie

CHARACTERS
DEREK – male, mid-30s, blue collar
MEL – female, mid-30s, blue collar

SETTING
The bedroom of a middle-class suburban couple. Christmas Eve.

For permission to produce this play, please contact the playwright at:
kitt@kittlavoie.com

Lights rise on the bedroom of a middle class suburban couple. Tubes of wrapping paper, ribbons, and other wrapping accoutrement are arrayed across the bed.

DEREK, mid-30s, is putting the finishing touches on the wrapping of a package. MEL, mid-30s, adds the package she has just finished wrapping to one of three piles of gifts at the center of the bed.

She digs into a crinkly plastic WAL-MART bag and pulls out a three-pack of Matchbox cars.

She turns to Derek, the color draining out of her face.

MEL   *(daunted)* That's it.

DEREK   That's it?

MEL   Mmm-hmm.

DEREK   Who's that one for?

MEL   Jarrod.

DEREK   Okay.

Derek goes back to wrapping.

MEL   How many is that?

Derek surveys the piles.

DEREK   That's... seven for Dave, seven for Brandi, and that'll be seven for Jarrod.

Mel sits hard on the edge of the bed.

MEL   It felt like more.

DEREK   It all feels like more this year.

Mel sits on the edge of the bed. She looks where she is sitting and shakes her head.

MEL   We couldn't sit on the edge of the bed last year. We could barely walk around in here last year.

Derek looks up and reaches for the Matchbox cars.

DEREK   Here.

Mel hands the Matchboxes to Derek. He rips open the package. He hands the three cars back to Mel.

DEREK   Wrap up one for each of them. Give the convertible to Brandi.

MEL   But now Dave and Brandi have eight and Jarrod only has seven.

DEREK   He's a big boy. He'll get it.

MEL   I don't know.

DEREK   They know I haven't been going to work. They'll be okay. They'll understand.

MEL   When Brandi gave me her Christmas list last week, I told her, "We're gonna have a small Christmas this year. Because of the business." You know what she said?

DEREK   What?

MEL   She said, "That's okay. Santa doesn't have a business. He has elves."

DEREK   Great. Then she'll be mad at Santa, not at us.

MEL   Derek–

DEREK I'm kidding. I'm kidding, Mel. They'll be fine. We'll have Christmas. We'll see your folks. They'll eat ham. They'll be fine.

Mel holds up the three loose Matchbox cars.

MEL We gave them a Wii last year.

DEREK And they're not getting one this year. They're getting everything we can give them this year. And it will be fine.

MEL I wish you would take this seriously.

DEREK I'm taking it—

MEL That's all I've wanted. Is for you to take this seriously, Derek.

DEREK Believe me, Mel, I'm taking it seriously. Look.

Derek picks up three wrapped packages – obviously books.

DEREK *(cont'd)* From my Aunt Laura. But— TADA!

He tears the labels off one of the packages and slaps a new label on it. He jots with a Sharpie and tosses it on one of the piles.

DEREK *(cont'd)* Nine. Fixed! It will be fine.

MEL How?

DEREK Because it will be. Because it has to be.

Mel just looks at him – "how do you not get this?"

She kneels down next to the bed and begins wrapping one of the Matchbox cars. Derek re-labels the other two books, then begins wrapping the second car. Mel finishes wrapping her car and moves on to the third one in silence. Derek finishes wrapping his car. With no more gifts to wrap, he watches her a moment.

He goes to the closet and pulls a large wrapped box from the top shelf. He places it on the bed in front of Mel.

DEREK *(cont'd)* I was going to save this until tomorrow...

MEL What is this?

DEREK It's nothing.

MEL What is this?

DEREK It's for you.

MEL Derek. We said no gifts.

DEREK I know.

MEL We said no gifts.

DEREK I know. It's Christmas.

MEL God damn it, Derek. I knew you'd do this.

DEREK Mel—

MEL We said no gifts because we can't afford any gifts. And you have never, ever understood anything like that. Never. Because everything is always going to be "fine," isn't it? It's fine to use the land as equity. It's fine to get the stainless-steel appliances. "Sure, Bill. The tile can wait 'til next week. That's just *fine*." And that is why they called in the loans. That is why the business failed. That is why we are in this mess to begin with. This thing you do. So don't "here's a present, it will be fine" and expect me to think it's sweet or generous or anything other than you being as irresponsible as you are always.

A long, cold silence.

DEREK   Open it.

MEL   I don't want it, whatever it is.

DEREK   *Open it.*

Mel just glowers at him. Derek advances and grabs the box from the bed. He tears the wrapping off, opens the box, and begins pulling out wads of colored tissue paper.

He reaches the bottom of the box and turns it over. Nothing comes out.

DEREK   *(cont'd)* It's nothing. I kept our deal. That was my present.

They stare at each other over the open package. Derek shakes his head.

DEREK   *(cont'd)* I thought it would be funny.

MEL   In what conceivable world would that be funny, Derek.

DEREK   You used to think I was funny.

Mel looks at the paltry pile of gifts on the bed.

MEL   Things just used to be funnier.

DEREK   I was trying. To make things better.

MEL   It's never for a lack of trying with you, Derek. It's always in the execution.

They look at each other a moment. Mel scoops up all the presents on the bed in one arm load and heads for the door.

MEL   *(cont'd)* Merry Christmas.

And she's gone.

Derek grabs the empty box and hurls it across the room. Being empty, it just sort of flops to the ground.

Derek looks after Mel for a moment, then gets on his knees and begins to finish wrapping the last Matchbox car.

Blackout.

END OF PLAY.

On the Edge of What Might Happen
by Sydney Painter

CHARACTERS
BEN – male, 4, excitable and genuine, played by an adult actor
ANDY – male, 3 ¾, a cool guy, played by an adult actor

SETTING
A suburban shopping mall

For permission to produce this play, please contact the playwright at:
sydney.painter@gmail.com

Note:
A "/" indicates an overlap.
"[ ]"s indicate the spirit of a thought not voiced.

BEN and ANDY are waiting in line, their eyes on the prize. Andy has more success than Ben at maintaining a façade of coolness.

BEN Dude.

ANDY I know.

BEN Like dude.

ANDY No I know.

BEN Like no dude for real though.

ANDY Dude you promised you'd be chill.

BEN I know but now that it's happening.

ANDY I know I know but you can't freak out ok.

BEN Ok.

ANDY You good?

BEN I'm good.

ANDY You got your list?

BEN Right here.

ANDY Ok. Now remember it's important to triage because he might cut you off. This is a busy mall.

BEN It's like not even about the presents at this point.

ANDY I know.

BEN		It's just like everything about him, man.
ANDY		He's a great man.
BEN		I cannot. Stop. Looking.
ANDY		Ok, it's ok to look/
BEN		That lap looks so freakin' cozy!
ANDY		Just settle yourself down, ok, my mom is watching.
BEN		So?
ANDY		So! I have asthma she worries about hyperventilation.
BEN		I don't have asthma.
ANDY		[Ok for real though] She'll start asking if we have to go to the bathroom.
BEN		Ooh rough.
ANDY		I know. Like I don't think of that.
BEN		I don't think of it usually.
ANDY		What the heck, Ben, you cannot say things like that.
BEN		Ok.
ANDY		Just cool it, ok? Be cool.
BEN		Ok.
ANDY		Ok.

Brief pause.

BEN	Can I go first?
ANDY	What? No.
BEN	I need to. I really need to.
ANDY	That's ridiculous. You are like actually speaking Chinese right now.
BEN	Andy, I've never asked you for anything.
ANDY	Um, yes you have. You asked me to bring you here. To this awesome suburban mall. To have an audience with Santa himself. And I made it happen for you.
BEN	My mom says guests get first pick.
ANDY	Oh does she.
BEN	Yup.
ANDY	Your mom says that.
BEN	Did I stutter?
ANDY	Well we aren't with your mom are we.
BEN	Uh–
ANDY	If we were with your mom we'd be lighting candles or some other nonsense for a fakey holiday that's not even mentioned in the old testament / dressed up to look like a present-giving occasion–
BEN	Whoa there Mel Gibson.
ANDY	–so they could take the same days off of work and their kids wouldn't feel left out of this totally awesome party that Jesus throws / every year.

BEN   Dude I wouldn't invoke Jesus right now—

ANDY   YOU WANTED CHRISTMAS. You wanted a tree and reindeer, and Santa's cozy, reassuring lap. And I brought you here even though you're kind of insulting your tribe.

BEN   Santa doesn't even have to do with Jesus! He's a Norse folk tale or something that Christians appropriated!

ANDY   I brought you, and we're with my mom. And my mom says I am a Christmas miracle. I was like eight months premature that's why my lungs are like soggy injera, and my birthday is next week so who do you think she's gonna let go first.

Pause.

BEN   How old are you.

ANDY   I'm three and three quarters, jerksock, I just told you my birthday's next week.

BEN   Well then that actually makes you three and fifty-one fifty-seconds—

ANDY   —Whoa whoa whoa I do not think there are that many fractions—

BEN   —And actually my birthday was two months ago. So.

ANDY   What are you saying.

BEN   I'm older.

ANDY   What. Did you just say to me.

BEN   I'm older than you.

ANDY   You're lying. There were no cupcakes at Teacher Laurie's. I never forget a cupcake.

BEN   My birthday is the day before Halloween so Teacher Laurie said I had to bring orange wedges because we were about to have so much candy the next day. Remember? Everyone was so sticky, and you got in trouble for giving Harper a dreadlock?

ANDY   Oh man. I do.

BEN   I'm older than you, and I'm sitting on that lap before you. I will only ask for my top fff–... six presents. I will speak loudly and clearly so as to minimize the prompting of repetition. And I will gaze into that beard until it is so awkward an elf lifts me down even though I am perfectly capable of sliding on my own, and she will set me so gently on my feet that my sneakers don't even flash. And then you can have your turn.

Brief pause.

ANDY   Fine.

BEN   Ok then.

ANDY   I didn't know you were older.

BEN   I don't like to have to use it.

ANDY   I didn't realize this meant that much to you.

BEN   Well I saw the Christmas episode of Lego Ninjago and the imagery is just caught in my mind, you know.

ANDY   Oh man, yeah, I saw that, it was powerful.

BEN   I just want to be a part of the Christmas magic.

ANDY That's beautiful, man.

BEN Thank you.

ANDY You're up.

Ben leaves the scene.

END OF PLAY.

Effigy
by Jennifer Reichert

CHARACTERS
NADINE – female, mid 30s, athletic and scruffy
ROBERT – male, late 30s, shaggy and rumpled

SETTING
A campsite in the Argentinean Andes, dusk

For permission to produce this play, please contact the playwright at:
jennifer@jenniferreichert.com

A campsite in the Argentinean Andes, with a tent nestled among hillocks of grass. A small fire burns in the firepit and the peaks of the Andes rise sharply behind.

NADINE, 36, athletic and scruffy, in a tank top and cargo pants, kneels on the ground stuffing tufts of grass into a scarecrow-like dummy. She surveys her handiwork, then sits the dummy up against a hillock. She walks forward and looks over the edge of a short cliff.

NADINE   What took you so long? The sun is setting. I finished the old man. Did you get me a surprise?

ROBERT   *(from below)* Hold your horses, I'll be right up. You had a long list.

She watches him from the cliff a moment. ROBERT, 39, shaggy and rumpled, in a yellow hoodie, comes into the campsite, panting. He shrugs off the pack and hoodie, and flings the hoodie over a grass hillock. He offers her the pack and she tosses him a canteen. He drinks deeply, while she rummages through the pack.

NADINE   Razor, soap, steaks, canned heat, scotch, mask.

ROBERT   They didn't have too many masks. I think that's supposed to be the president.

Nadine puts the mask on the stuffed man.

NADINE   That'll work. Did you get the fireworks? M-80s?

ROBERT   In the paper bag. Are you sure about all those fireworks? With the grass?

NADINE   I built up the fire ring, dug the pit down, and cleared the grass back further. And I got buckets of water. We wait for midnight, put the *viejo* in the firepit, and set him on fire!

ROBERT   So the most important thing we're rid of from this year is the president of Argentina?

NADINE Well it's the only mask they had left, right? Burning your political leaders is pretty standard, I think. National embarrassments. But it can be personal too. Your boss, your mother-in-law, ya know, out with the old. I gave our old man those scratchy socks that gave you that awful blister. And his hands are the red socks that ruined my favorite white shirt. Plus I had, ya know, *thoughts* of 2015 while stuffing him. Good riddance, 2015!

Robert digs into the bag and pulls out and holds up a bag of fun size Snickers.

NADINE *(cont'd)* Oh my god! Real Snickers! That must have cost you a fortune.

ROBERT Well, there's only one day left. Happy New Year's Eve!

Robert brings her the Snickers and leans down to kiss her soundly.

NADINE Happy New Year's Eve to you too. *(beat)* Let's put the fireworks in the *viejo*!

She grabs the paper bag and the stuffed man and starts shoving fireworks inside the grass stuffing.

ROBERT It's New Year's tomorrow.

NADINE Yes.

ROBERT And the next day we're leaving. Hiking down to Mendoza and flying back to the States.

NADINE Yes.

ROBERT We should talk. About that. About where we're going. We kept saying we'd talk about it tomorrow. There's no more tomorrows left.

Nadine stops stuffing fireworks and sits back, looking at him.

NADINE   I know.

ROBERT   I don't want this to end.

NADINE   Me either. But we have to.

Nadine crawls over and kisses him.

ROBERT   Fly to Seattle with me. Move in with me.

NADINE   Whoa. No.

ROBERT   Why not?

NADINE   It's too fast. I'm not moving to Seattle. We've never even gone on a date.

ROBERT   We've shared a tent for five months. I'd say we've moved past dinner and a movie.

NADINE   No we haven't. We've never been to a movie.

ROBERT   We've crossed four borders. We fell into a ravine. We almost died together on that suspension bridge. And again, we sleep in the same tent. So I think we've skipped ahead in the whole courtship ritual.

NADINE   Which might be fine if we were planning to live here. But we don't live here. This is an interlude. Let's just enjoy what we've had. I wish it didn't have to end, but it's time to go back to our lives.

ROBERT   Or we could continue enjoying it together.

NADINE   Back where we really live, we are at basically zero. I don't know what you're like there.

ROBERT   You know everything about me.

NADINE   I don't think I do. And how important is the stuff I do know about you, back in civilization? This has been fun–

ROBERT   Fun? It's been fun?!

NADINE   –but it can't be sustained in a place where we have, like, modern world responsibilities. It's been amazing up here. It was a good thing. Let's not ruin it. I want to remember it.

ROBERT   And how would it be ruined by keeping it going?

NADINE   I don't want to be disappointed. I couldn't take disappointing you.

ROBERT   You wouldn't.

NADINE   I'm not a magical mountain nymph, Robert. I'm a human woman.

Nadine eyes Robert's yellow hoodie.

NADINE   *(cont'd)* I should put something more on.

She picks it up. He stiffens.

NADINE   *(cont'd)* Can I wear this? *(beat)* You don't mind, right?

ROBERT   It's fine.

NADINE   No it's not. You never let me wear this hoodie. You don't want me to wear this one because your ex-wife gave it to you.

ROBERT   She didn't give it to me. I borrowed it and never gave it back.

NADINE   So give it back to her.

She tosses the hoodie at him. She pulls a sweatshirt out of the tent and puts it on. He puts on the hoodie.

NADINE *(cont'd)* Or get rid of it.

ROBERT I can't.

NADINE Can't get rid of it or can't give it back? Because you want to keep it?

ROBERT She asked for it back.

NADINE And you didn't give it. I have no idea what kind of relationship you have with her back there. You might still be hung up on her. You hang onto things. You hang onto things of hers. We don't have a relationship where we know everything about our exes. Our whole relationship is up here. Let's just let it be here, as it was. Please.

ROBERT I was married to her for 12 years. Lisa is part of who I am. Was.

NADINE And you want me to move in to the house you lived in with her? I can't move to Seattle, into that same house. So you can run into her and return her hoodie? So you can have doubts and we get driven apart?

ROBERT I know that you are the person I want to be with.

NADINE You can say that here. But how do I know that?

ROBERT Because I say it. It's you. You're tough and loyal and you see beauty everywhere, in the smallest things. Forget Seattle, we can go to Chicago. I'll move in to your place.

NADINE I don't have a place anymore. I had to move out of my place when I broke up with Brett. Another thing

NADINE   *(cont'd)* you didn't know about me.

ROBERT   I knew that. I just meant Chicago.

NADINE   And I'm not flying back to Chicago. I've spent seven months letting go of everything from my life before. Job, apartment, friends who only know me as Brett's girlfriend, habits. Everything I could I let go of. I'm going home. Do you even know where home is?

ROBERT   No. I don't. But I want to. Tell me. Where's home?

NADINE   No. I'm not telling you like this. What are you going to do? Follow me there? I've let go, Robert. It's time.

ROBERT   Why would you want to let go of this? I want to hold on to this! This is more than just a mountain hook-up. Didn't it mean anything to you?

NADINE   Of course it means something to me! But when we go back, we're going to have jobs, and family obligations, and rents – or a mortgage? Real-real life is not the same as this life. Do you have a mortgage?

Robert shakes his head. Nadine flops down in front of the tent, her hand to her mouth.

NADINE   Shoot.

ROBERT   That's disappointing? I could if I wanted to, I guess.

NADINE   Shoot shoot shoot.

Nadine sighs and reaches into the tent. She pulls out a zipper pouch, unzips it and pulls out a syringe and vial. She fills the syringe from the vial, lifts her shirt and injects herself in the belly. He watches, stunned.

NADINE   *(cont'd)* I'm diabetic. That's real life.

ROBERT This whole time— For five months, I've never seen you...

NADINE No. Because I hid it. One thing I couldn't let go of. But I wasn't going to let it slow me down. And I didn't want you to treat me like I was some delicate... whatever.

ROBERT This is serious.

NADINE Yes. But this wasn't real life. I didn't need to "disclose." I hid it. Who knows what else you've kept hidden? To "protect" me. Or yourself.

She puts the syringe away, then reaches for the bag of Snickers. She tears it open with her teeth and takes out one and holds it in her hand, waiting.

NADINE *(cont'd)* You have an ex-wife who's still important to you. And shared friends. Back there. That's real life. I can't try to fit into your old life. I want a new real life. Our time up here has been the best thing in the last three years for me. I really needed this trip. I needed you.

ROBERT What if the trip didn't end? What if we kept going and go somewhere new?

NADINE But you're tied there. Your life is with other people who aren't me.

ROBERT It doesn't have to be.

She sighs, and eats the Snickers. Then she goes to the viejo *and starts stuffing him with more fireworks.*

NADINE I used the last of the stroganoff packs for our dinner tonight.

ROBERT Nadine—

NADINE We have the scotch for drinks. Snickers for dessert. We have three more hours 'til midnight and then we burn the old man.

ROBERT That's enough fireworks. We're trying to burn an effigy, not start a fracking operation.

Nadine keeps stuffing the fireworks in. Robert kneels down next to her and stops her. She looks at him.

NADINE You want too much. We had this. This was good. We should move on. And keep this special. Please I need it to stay good. I need just one to stay good, one that doesn't end in flames, or ashes. Let me keep this one.

He arranges the old man's clothes. She takes out a sharpie and writes "2015" across the chest.

NADINE *(cont'd)* This was the one good thing in a disastrous year. And I need to put this year behind me.

ROBERT You don't want enough. We can keep this and make it more.

NADINE What if we kept going, and it all gets worn away? I couldn't take that. It would break me.

She walks over to the cliff and looks down at the town. Robert follows her.

ROBERT It's not going to wear away.

NADINE I wouldn't be enough and – You have a whole life there. You have strong ties there. You're not like me. I don't think you can let go. And that's ok, it's really ok.

ROBERT I can. I want to. I will.

NADINE Saying it doesn't make it true.

He walks over and inspects the viejo. *He wrestles off his yellow hoodie and struggles to fit it onto the old man. She looks over and sees the hoodie on the* viejo. *He hoists the old man up and strides to the fire.*

NADINE *(cont'd)* What are you doing? It's not midnight yet.

ROBERT It is somewhere. We're starting the New Year now. Good riddance, 2015.

He flings the old man into the flames. The yellow hoodie blackens as flames engulf the viejo.

ROBERT *(cont'd)* I'm ready to go. Wherever you want.

Nadine stares into the flames, as they leap high in the air, cracking.

ROBERT *(cont'd)* I want a new real life, too, Nadine. And I want it with you.

Nadine looks up from the fire. She turns to Robert.

NADINE Home is Santa Monica. *(beat)*

ROBERT I hear it's beautiful.

NADINE It is. You'll love it.

He pulls her close and they kiss. The flames detonate in a crescendo of exploding fireworks.

END OF PLAY.

Year After Year
by Mélisa Breiner-Sanders

CHARACTERS
MARY – female, 50s, motherly
PAUL – male, 50s, problem solver

SETTING
Christmas time

For permission to produce this play, please contact the playwright at:
BreinerSandersProductions@gmail.com or Melisa@MelisaBS.com

We see a living room modestly decorated for Christmas: a one-foot Christmas tree with lights and a star on top sits in the corner, a poinsettia is at the door and various other decorations are scattered. A box of decorations remains half unpacked and to the side. There is a warm, soft glow to the room. MARY, *50s, is beginning to set the table.*

PAUL, also 50s, enters and begins to take off his layers. He holds a shopping bag.

PAUL	The stores weren't nearly as bad as I thought they'd be but the shelves were just about emptied out. Still able to get milk but only a pint.
MARY	That's fine, we won't be need more than that anyway.

Paul puts the milk in the fridge and looks over to Mary.

PAUL	What are you doing?
MARY	Setting the table.
PAUL	You know what I mean.
MARY	...I'm just setting the table.
PAUL	Don't do that.
MARY	Don't do what?
PAUL	Please, Mary, just stop.
MARY	Would *you* rather set the table?
PAUL	No, I would not rather set the table.
MARY	Because you can certainly set the table if you don't want me to set the table.

PAUL Can we stop saying, "set the table"?! *(beat)* I thought we were past this.

MARY Past what?

PAUL You don't see what you're doing?

MARY I'm cooking dinner, I've decorated, I'm setting the–

PAUL I never asked you to decorate, I could have done that.

MARY I wanted to.

PAUL And now we see how well that's worked out.

A quick beat.

MARY I think it all looks nice.

PAUL Look at what you're doing.

MARY What?!

PAUL You're setting the table for three.

Mary looks down at the table, takes a moment and realizes what she did. She deflates.

MARY Shit.

PAUL This is bad...

MARY It'll be fine.

PAUL How is it going to be fine?

MARY I don't do it on purpose... It's... muscle memory and sometimes it just happens.

PAUL   After six years it shouldn't.

MARY   I didn't realize there was a time limit.

PAUL   There's no time limit but at some point...

MARY   At some point what?

PAUL   At some point we... have to... I don't know.

MARY   You don't know...

PAUL   I just want you to be better.

MARY   By forgetting her?

PAUL   Being better doesn't mean you forget.

MARY   It does to you.

PAUL   It does not.

MARY   It does. Every time I remember her, you get upset.

PAUL   If you told stories or looked at pictures or... this is something else.

MARY   You've forgotten.

PAUL   I have not. How dare you.

MARY   You have. You never speak about her, I always have to be the one to—

PAUL   Just because I don't go around crying about it all the time doesn't mean it's not there. Not all of us have to advertise. Sometimes things are private.

MARY   Private from me?

PAUL	How am I supposed to talk to you?
MARY	With your words...
PAUL	I can't. I don't know what it will happen if I talk about her. I walk in that door and I never know what to expect.
MARY	That's not true.
PAUL	Some days are fine and then some days you cry non-stop and then some days you've dragged her tennis racket out of storage and put it by the front door like she's coming home from school.
MARY	I'm doing the best that I can.
PAUL	It's just... when things are good with you, I don't want to ruin it.
MARY	You won't ruin it. *(beat)* When we talk about her, it's like some part of her is here. It's nice.

A few beats.

PAUL	I don't know if that's good or bad for you...

A few more beats.

MARY	You have to stop hiding things from me.
PAUL	I know, you want me to talk about–
MARY	Not thoughts. Things.
PAUL	Oh.

A beat.

MARY I found her stocking today. I saw it and I just stared at it and thought, "What am I supposed to do with this?" Do I put it up? Do I throw it away? Do I put it back in the box like it doesn't exist? Paul clearly thought it was better to hide it. But now I *know* it's here, I can't forget I know it's here and then it just feels like I'm ignoring her if I put it away, like she's no longer part of the family. So I put it aside to figure it out later and then I see the old Christmas cards. You always hated that I saved them, said it was pointless and it was all just junk Janey would have to go through when we passed so better for us to throw it out now to save her the trouble.

A few beats.

PAUL Did you find the angel?

MARY Where is it?

PAUL I put it in a box labeled "More Bows."

MARY But I labeled that box.

PAUL That's why I knew you wouldn't check in there.

Paul goes to the large cardboard box filled with multiple smaller boxes. He has an idea where it is and searches.

MARY Where are the bows?

PAUL Why do we need two boxes of bows?

MARY They were still good.

PAUL There was four layers of tape on the back and they were all smushed down. If you really want, I can get a whole new bag at the dollar store.

MARY IT JUST SEEMS WASTEFUL.

PAUL   Here it is.

He finds the box labeled "More Bows" and reverently brings it to the table. He opens the box to find an angel tree topper that has seen many years of use but has been flattened because of its time in the box. Paul takes it out and hands it to Mary. Mary stares at it and unconsciously begins to fix it up.

MARY   She wanted to look just like this angel.

They both just stare at it.

PAUL   Let's put it on the tree.

Mary nods, rises, and moves towards the tree in the corner. The angel is too big for the small tree and most of the angel has to lean against the wall to be upright. She takes out a bulb from the string of lights, plugs in the angel and she glows. Paul and Mary stare at the tree, just far apart from each other so as not to touch. Mary begins to cry. Paul gingerly puts his arm around her shoulders as the lights fade to black.

END OF PLAY.

Believin'
by Sharon E. Cooper

CHARACTERS
STEPHANIE – female, 30s, quirky, a dog walker
SELENA – female, 40s, Rothchild's wife, elegant
ROTHCHILD – male, 40s, Selena's husband, trying to do the right thing

SETTING
A suburban home on New Year's Eve, the present

For permission to produce this play, please contact the playwright at:
www.sharonecooper.com or secooper1@yahoo.com

An upper-middle class home somewhere in suburban America. New Year's Eve. Way after midnight.

SELENA, late 40s, dressed elegantly in a silk pants suit, finishes a glass of wine and walks across a beautifully furnished living room, away from ROTHCHILD, late 40s. Neither of them sees STEPHANIE, late 30s, sitting in a chair in the corner of the room. Stephanie dips a carrot and watches them like she's watching a movie. Rothchild follows Selena across the room.

SELENA   I almost fell into the toilet. I could have ruined my dress.

ROTHCHILD Everyone's gone. You *could have* changed.

SELENA   Should I put on a wet suit in my own home *just in case?*

ROTHCHILD It's not a bathtub. It's the size of a toilet.

SELENA   It is a toilet!

ROTHCHILD Exactly!

SELENA   Exactly!

ROTHCHILD And how did you know it was *me?* There were a lot of men here tonight.

SELENA   But only one is always here. Only one, for sure, always leaves the toilet seat up.

ROTHCHILD I'm going to go help in the kitchen.

SELENA   Help whom? No one is in the kitchen.

ROTHCHILD *(storming out)* Exactly.

SELENA   *(yelling after him)* And I already cleaned up the kitchen. You're welcome!

She waits. From the other room: Silence... Stephanie emerges out of the shadows.

STEPHANIE Ebola.

Selena jumps and catches her breath.

SELENA Oh– God. Sorry– I–

STEPHANIE That's what I was just thinking about right now. I think that's going to be the end of all of us, Ebola. I love this dip. Great party.

Selena takes a good look at Stephanie and...

SELENA So – so it's getting so – late – and it's so hard at these parties that you don't get to talk to everyone–

STEPHANIE And I'm so glad you waited till everyone left so we wouldn't be interrupted because I'd like to talk to you and Rothchild about–

SELENA *(calling out)* Rothchild. *(He doesn't come back, so she screams)* Rothchild!

Rothchild enters, his arms folded. He doesn't see Stephanie.

ROTHCHILD There would be no point in my doing the dishes because you're always correcting me – whether it's–

SELENA *(indicating Stephanie)* You remember – uh, ah–

ROTHCHILD Oh, um–

STEPHANIE Now that we're all here together, *finally*–

ROTHCHILD Who are you?

STEPHANIE I feel the same way Rothchild. Like who are we? Why are we here? What are we meant to–

ROTHCHILD No, I meant it more literally.

STEPHANIE Oh. Stephanie. I sometimes go by Strawfanie. But recently just Stephanie. Here.

Stephanie hands Selena a "Stella's Shoes" bag.

SELENA How – thoughtful – what a nice – what is it?

STEPHANIE Raymond. He– he died.

Selena drops the bag. Rothchild starts laughing. Stephanie lunges, grabs the bag and takes out an urn and cradles it.

SELENA *(to Rothchild)* This isn't funny.

STEPHANIE No, it's not.

ROTHCHILD Bringing an urn to a New Year's Eve party? It's a little funny.

SELENA Because you're the expert on mourning etiquette?

ROTHCHILD I was *trying*.

SELENA Maybe next year Strawfanie will get lucky and you'll throw her a party on–

ROTHCHILD *Strawfanie* is not my wife.

SELENA Maybe you should have asked your wife if she'd like to host a hundred people on the first anniversary of her father's death.

ROTHCHILD You said you wanted a distraction.

SELENA A distraction is a massage or getting a pedicure, not filling everyone's wine glass while you sit in the other room all night watching television.

ROTHCHILD How could I be watching television in one room and plotting against you, a.k.a. the toilet seat lifter, all at the same time?

STEPHANIE *(interjecting)* My name's actually just Stephanie, not Strawfanie! I just said that because of Phil.

ROTHCHILD Who's Phil?

STEPHANIE Phil was this guy – that I don't care about at all – after we broke up three months ago, I moved five hundred miles away so he wouldn't have to be upset if he ever ran into me. In our bedroom. Or at Phyllis's grave. So I wish you two would stop arguing about toilets and televisions and start acting like *(picking up a picture from the mantle)* these people in your getting married outfits because I'm not leaving until we give Raymond a proper funeral!

ROTHCHILD Perhaps you would like the name of the folks we used—

SELENA Rothchild, everyone mourns differently. You can't blame her for—

ROTHCHILD For having a "Surprise!" "Funeral!" in my house for some *(leaning into Selena and loud whispering)* loony tune I don't even know—

STEPHANIE Raymond loved Echo and Lovely like his brothers. I have the holiday card of *(indicating Rothchild and Selena)* you and you and Echo and Lovely on the fridge. So I'm someone who knows you. Or at least I thought I did.

SELENA The dog walker! You're the dog walker! Raymond is a dog!

STEPHANIE Raymond is – was – a cat. Do you realize how lucky you were that I brought him over here to build

STEPHANIE *(cont'd)* bridges across animal lines? Raymond and Echo and Lovely would run around this very room, chasing each other's tails, chasing their own tails, and I would look at these nice pictures of these nice people skiing and surfing and laughing and wearing matching red sweaters with their dogs! And it was worth it, even though I had to bring my own *baggies*, even though I only make $15 an hour, not even $18 – and when I work for a Rothchild–

ROTHCHILD My name's Rothchild. I'm not *a* Rothschild.

STEPHANIE Tomato, tomato. *(beat)* Come on, people – please – start acting like the happy people with the happy dogs!

SELENA Those pictures were from a long time ago.

ROTHCHILD It's because I leave the toilet seat up...

SELENA Because you leave me to take care of everything.

STEPHANIE Maybe I should just cancel the funeral. I'll take Raymond home and mourn him in my small three-room house, just a few blocks away from your McMansion. Or maybe I'll just see if I can get some people to "like" my funeral on Facebook.

ROTHCHILD Oh for heaven's sake, we could, you know, say a prayer.

STEPHANIE I mean, if you want. If it would give you closure. Let us pray. Wait. Don't you think you should get Echo and Lovely?

SELENA They're not that religious. And they're at my cousins. Rothchild wanted the house to be dog free.

ROTHCHILD For our allergic friends.

SELENA Right, but then I had to drive them to my cousins.

ROTHCHILD I don't have cousins nearby.

SELENA But you do drive, right?

ROTHCHILD I was working.

SELENA I had to take off work to bring them over and get back in time to host a party on the anniversary of my father's death.

STEPHANIE Well, I guess we should go ahead and get started before Raymond's been dead too long. One of you should start.

Selena nudges Rothchild to speak.

ROTHCHILD Raymond was like a dog walker-in-law to me... And in-laws matter. When they die – it's a loss to you, too, you know. Amen.

SELENA Maybe Raymond just wanted to be with Strawfanie. Like it used to be in the beginning. When they would sit in a car with a bottle of cheap wine and look at the stars.

STEPHANIE We never did that.

ROTHCHILD Maybe he didn't always show it, but I think Raymond was lucky to have Echo and Lovely all of those years.

STEPHANIE Months. Three months. And thank you both. That was really, really touching.

ROTHCHILD Well, you're like family. And we're happy to refer you to other families. In the next town.

SELENA *(to Rothchild)* Or we'll pay her $18 instead of $15 and include a holiday bonus.

ROTHCHILD Yes, yes, of course. If that's what you want.

STEPHANIE L'chaim. I accept. Raymond would appreciate it. Raymond was Zoroastrian, but I never learned what that meant and he would want me to say a prayer in my own faith tradition, just as you did. He was a universalist in that way. *(looking up)* Dear Cat Heaven – please accept Raymond into your fold. Fold him into the floating clouds. He was a model to us all. He never got Botox even though his face sagged a little. Let him enjoy being with Phyllis, Phil's dog – that Bastard – Phil, not the dog, whom he shared so many great memories. We hope Phil burns in Hell even though he doesn't believe in Hell. *(composing herself)* I hope that Echo and Lovely won't join Raymond for a long, long time in Heaven. But if you see it fit to kill Phil, I think everyone would understand.

Rothchild and Selena look at each other. Maybe she's done?

STEPHANIE *(cont'd)* And Raymond, I won't change my email address. I promise. I'll always be raymondandme1@yahoo.com and I'll use your name as a password even if it leaves a big empty hole inside me every time I order mascara online. Maybe I won't even wear make-up anymore. You taught me that I should just be me and accept me and my face just as I am, which gets harder when everyone at New Year's Eve looks like the same person because they've all had Botox... Sometimes you live. Sometimes you love. Sometimes you get to have both. I will miss you Raymond... I thought I would have at least been divorced by now...

Stephanie picks up a picture from Rothchild and Selena's wedding day.

STEPHANIE *(cont'd)* This was your dad?

SELENA *(looking)* Yeah, he was about to walk me down the aisle and I leaned over and said – "I think I'm making a good decision" and he said "a great decision." And then I walked down the aisle and vowed to be with Rothchild for better or worse.

ROTHCHILD I would like to make a new vow. On the anniversary of my father-in-law's death. Since I haven't put the toilet seat down consistently for fifteen years, for the next fifteen, I will. After that, we can negotiate.

SELENA And I won't complain about how you clean the dishes. Just rinse them before you put them in the dishwasher. And you can ask more questions about what I really want... And I want to know more about what my dad meant to you, like I want details.

ROTHCHILD How could you not know that?

SELENA I don't know.

ROTHCHILD Sounds like a great conversation over New Year's Day brunch.

He puts his arms around her. She lets him.

STEPHANIE *(singing)* "I'm just a small town girl. Living in a lonely world. Took the midnight train going anywhere." *(sobbing)* I'm fine. That was our song. It's hard to sing it without Raymond. He had a beautiful meow. *(singing)* "Some will win; some will lose. Some will all sing the blues. Took the midnight train going anywhere."

ROTHCHILD *(to Selena)* Next year, just you and me.

SELENA And maybe Echo and Lovely. And–

She looks over at Stephanie.

ROTHCHILD We'll see.

SELENA Sure.

STEPHANIE Are you all going to sing along or– *(They nod. She sings.)* "Don't stop– believing."

ALL *(singing)* "Hold on to that feeling. Streetlights. People. Oooohhhhoooo..."

"Don't Stop Believin'" plays as they toast to Raymond and to life as the lights fade.

END OF PLAY.

Please note, *the author does not own the rights to "Don't Stop Believin'." If productions are unable to obtain the rights, the author suggests substituting "God Bless America" (which is in the public domain) with the lyrics "meowed" by Stephanie, Selena, and Rothchild.*

IRL
by Will Clark

CHARACTERS
BRETT – a young man, 25
SUSAN – a young mother, 32

SETTING
Inside Brett's Buick

For permission to produce this play, please contact the playwright at:
wclark1018@gmail.com

Lights up. BRETT, *mid-20s, sits in his car smoking a cigarette.*

BRETT Shhhhhhhhhhhhhhhhoot.

He reaches down to turn on the radio. The sound of Johnny Mercer crooning "Baby It's Cold Outside" bursts through the speakers. He immediately shuts it off.

BRETT *(cont'd, muttering)* Shoot, shoot, shoot, shoot, shoot...

He checks his mirror again, abruptly sits upright in his seat, and hurriedly takes one last puff before tossing it out the window. Brett reaches across to the passenger door and swings it open.

SUSAN Are you crazy?

SUSAN, early-30s, climbs into the passenger seat and slams the door shut violently.

BRETT I know.

SUSAN No seriously, are you crazy?

BRETT No. Look, can I–

SUSAN My house?

BRETT I know. It's... weird.

SUSAN Weird? It's terrifying.

BRETT Oh, I don't know about–

SUSAN How the hell am I supposed to explain this away? Do you have any idea of the crap that comes out of a six-year-old's mouth at the dinner table?

BRETT I didn't think of that. I'm sorry.

SUSAN What if Ted was home?

BRETT I thought of that.

SUSAN What?

BRETT I waited until he wasn't.

SUSAN You watched my house and waited?

BRETT Um. Yeah. I. Yeah.

SUSAN *How do you even know where I live?*

BRETT The polar bear. You mentioned the inflatable polar bear. And you had already told me you lived around Hyde Park. I just... I was driving through the area the other day and it caught my eye. And I thought, "Is that her house?" I guess I just got curious. So I looked around and, well... there aren't a lot of other people with inflatable polar bears in their yards over here. None actually.

SUSAN You do realize how insane this is.

BRETT It's not like we never talked about the chances of this happening.

SUSAN We talked about what it would be like if we ran into each other. We never talked about what it would be like if you sat outside my house, waiting for my *husband* to leave, so that you could knock on my door and introduce yourself to my *daughter*.

BRETT That part was an accident.

A beat.

SUSAN You know what? You aren't crazy. I'm crazy.

Susan opens her door to leave. Brett reaches out for her arm.

BRETT   Suz...

Susan whips around. Brett releases her arm, raising his hands and surrendering.

BRETT   *(cont'd)* I'm still just me.

Susan softens a bit. She closes the door. They both sit in silence for a minute.

BRETT   *(cont'd)* You sound different than I imagined. *(beat)* I know this is a little... odd.

SUSAN   That was pretty stupid Brett.

BRETT   Yeah. Probably. I just know the holidays can be tough. For both of us.

SUSAN   Are you alright?

BRETT   Yeah. Yeah, I'm okay.

SUSAN   Good.

BRETT   What about you? You doin' okay? I've been worried about you.

SUSAN   Yeah. I'm... good.

BRETT   I don't believe you.

Silence.

SUSAN   I have to get back to the house.

BRETT   You just got here. You can't spare a few minutes.

SUSAN   *(curt)* No, I really can't. *(beat)* I'm sorry. This doesn't work.

BRETT   I'm sorry. I didn't mean to make it weird.

SUSAN　　　No, I'm making it weird now.

BRETT　　　Yeah.

An awkward silence. Brett reaches into his pocket and pulls out his phone. He types a brief text message and tentatively places the phone on the dashboard. Susan looks at the phone and looks at Brett who smiles sheepishly.

SUSAN　　　Brett...

Brett shrugs, and turns away. Susan picks up the phone and reads his message. She takes a deep breath before typing a response and, apologetically, places the phone back on the dashboard.

Brett picks up the phone and checks her response. He crumbles slightly. Shaking his head, he rapidly types a response, placing it back on the dash.

Susan retrieves the phone again. She types what is clearly a one word answer, and defiantly places the phone on the dashboard.

BRETT　　　(cont'd) You could have both you know.

Brett picks up the phone off the dash and types again. He tries to hand her the phone, but she holds up her hands defensively.

SUSAN　　　No Brett!

Brett, crestfallen, places the phone on the dash once more. Susan, exhausted by the charade, snatches it up and reads.

SUSAN　　　(cont'd) No you didn't.

BRETT　　　It's nothing special, it's... here.

Brett reaches into the back seat and comes back holding a small, neatly wrapped package.

BRETT　　　(cont'd) Merry Christmas.

SUSAN　　　I can't.

BRETT   Sure you can. Go ahead, open it.

She opens the package and pulls out an ornament.

BRETT   *(cont'd)* Just something to hang on the tree. I figured if you were feeling a little down, or lonely... you know, you could look at it and... yeah, I don't know. You're the only person I know that I actually felt deserved a gift from me this year.

Susan looks out the window, back toward her house.

BRETT   *(cont'd)* You haven't logged on in over a month.

SUSAN   I know. I told you, I can't keep doing this.

BRETT   I thought I was helping.

SUSAN   You were. You were helping me. Not Ted. Not *us*. I need to be thinking about him, instead of leaving him to deal with our problems on his own. And that means not retreating to my computer every time we are supposed to crawl in bed together.

BRETT   Is it working? Are things getting better?

SUSAN   I'm trying.

BRETT   Well we don't have to talk at night. I mean, we don't even have to talk about him.

Silence. After a long beat.

BRETT   *(cont'd)* A goodbye would have been nice. I think after two years I've earned at least that.

SUSAN   Well maybe this will have to be it. *(pause)* I'm sorry.

BRETT   No I'm sorry. I shouldn't have come. That was stupid.

SUSAN   It's not that. I just... I need to make this change for myself right now.

BRETT   I see. I mean I understand. Just promise me if you need me you will come back.

Susan looks away from Brett. She picks up the ornament out of her lap and hangs it from his rearview mirror. She leans toward him and kisses him on the cheek. After a moment, she opens the door to leave.

BRETT   *(cont'd)* Suz... don't be afraid to tell him your feelings. They're perfect.

Susan smiles.

SUSAN   It was good meeting you Brett. It... it made my Christmas.

BRETT   Mine too.

Susan opens the door and exits. Brett looks up at the ornament hanging from his mirror, watching Susan disappear into her house.

Blackout.

END OF PLAY.

Isle of View
by Jerzy Gwiazdowski

CHARACTERS
GLORIA – female, 70s, wistful and creative
ANTHONY – male, 80, doting and kind

SETTING
A modest living room in small-town Minnesota

For permission to produce this play, please contact the playwright at:
jerzygwiazdowski@cryhavoccompany.org

A living room. Small-town Minnesota. Post-war American middle-class furnishings and Christmas decorations. A Christmas tree with flower garland hanging across, a hula figure on top, and a grass skirt on the bottom. Bing Crosby and the Andrews Sisters' version of "Mele Kalikimaka" plays on a turntable.

GLORIA, late 70s, sits in her chair next to the couch, drinking an eggnog Mai Tai. ANTHONY, 80, does a little hula dance as the song finishes. Gloria applauds. Anthony removes the 45rpm single from the record player and places it in a sleeve. Anthony dances over to Gloria. He reaches for the glass in her hand. Gloria places her other hand on top of his.

GLORIA Wait.

Anthony stops.

GLORIA (cont'd) I don't want you to leave.

ANTHONY I'm not going anywhere. Just to the kitchen.

GLORIA But when I don't see you, I fall apart.

ANTHONY I'll be right back.

GLORIA Seriously?

ANTHONY Seriously, seriously.

Anthony kisses the top of her head. He heads to the kitchen with the empty glass. Gloria reaches under the cushion of her chair and produces a slightly smushed roll of paper tied up with a ribbon. She places it in her lap.

Anthony re-enters with a box of cookies. Gloria extends her paper roll to him.

ANTHONY (cont'd) What's this?

GLORIA It's Christmas Eve. And you're flying me to Hawaii. I got you something in return.

ANTHONY   My only present is your presence. And maybe a few coconut macaroons?

Anthony shakes the box enticingly.

GLORIA   I don't want any.

ANTHONY   But they're your favorite: "True Chew Coconut Macaroons!"

GLORIA   How can they be? I've never had them before. Will you please open my gift?

ANTHONY   I think you've had these before. You recognize the box they come in, don't you?

Anthony holds the box toward Gloria. She isn't interested.

GLORIA   No. This is important. I want you to have it.

Gloria holds out her rolled paper gift. Anthony looks at it. He puts the cookie box down.

ANTHONY   I'm glad to be back, Gloria. I've missed you.

GLORIA   Then open it.

Anthony takes the smushed paper gift.

ANTHONY   Are you sure you don't want a cookie?

GLORIA   Anthony.

ANTHONY   ...Alright.

He undoes the ribbon and unrolls the paper. He looks at it.

GLORIA   Anthony. I'm so glad you're here. I was worried about you while you were away.

ANTHONY But I'm alright, Gloria. I'm here now. You see me, right?

GLORIA I'm so glad to see you. All I wanted was to see you. And I couldn't. And I thought I might never see you again. So I drew this.

Anthony looks at the picture.

GLORIA *(cont'd)* It's our own private island. It's a place we'll always be together, even when we're apart. So, now you'll always have it. If you have to go away again. Just open it up and know that I'm there. You can see me. And I can see you.

ANTHONY Gloria. Thank you.

GLORIA I want you to know I'm with you. I know 1953 has been hard. But 1954 will be different.

Anthony looks at the picture. He kisses the top of Gloria's head.

ANTHONY Gloria. I have something for you, too.

GLORIA Don't go.

ANTHONY I'll be right back.

GLORIA Seriously?

ANTHONY Seriously, Seriously.

He exits. Gloria looks at her drawing. Anthony returns, holding a picture frame. He hands it to her. She looks at it.

GLORIA You drew this for me?

ANTHONY No. You drew it for me. In 1953. It hangs in our hallway over there.

Gloria extends the frame toward Andrew.

GLORIA You're already taking me to Hawaii. I can't accept another gift.

ANTHONY Gloria. We aren't flying to Hawaii. We already went. Quite a few years ago. Do you remember that?

GLORIA We're not going?

ANTHONY We can't.

GLORIA Do you have to go back to Korea?

ANTHONY Gloria, I need you to understand. It isn't 1953. Nineteen fifty-three was a long time ago.

GLORIA But you just got back.

ANTHONY Yes – I did just get back, but I wasn't in Korea, Gloria. I was in the hospital. Korea was a long time ago. I had to go away to the doctor. But I'm back now.

GLORIA I'm glad you're back. When I don't see you, I fall apart.

ANTHONY Do you remember drawing this picture before?

GLORIA No.

ANTHONY Do you remember the last time I had to leave for a little while? You did it then, too. And Craig is getting worried. He thinks it's time for us to move.

GLORIA Who?

ANTHONY Craig. Our son. He's worried. He wants to be sure we're safe. He's worried about me, too. Do you remember? He came to see us a few weeks ago.

GLORIA   Craig?

Anthony picks up the box of cookies and hands it to Gloria.

ANTHONY   Craig brought cookies for us. He makes cookies. He makes a lot of cookies. The kind you buy at the grocery store. See this? "Savor, Steadfast, True Chews" Coconut Macaroons. Your favorite. He makes these. You do recognize the box, don't you?

Gloria holds the box, turning it over in her hands. She stares at the back of the box.

ANTHONY   *(cont'd)* That's his photograph on the back.

GLORIA   *(looking up at Anthony)* Craig. This is Craig.

ANTHONY   Yes. You remember?

GLORIA   I do. When I see him. I need to see him. I forget when I don't see him.

Gloria holds onto the box.

ANTHONY   You're going to see him. He's going to come back tomorrow. And he's going to help us move. Somewhere new.

GLORIA   We're going to move tomorrow?

ANTHONY   Yes.

GLORIA   On Christmas Day? What about dinner?

ANTHONY   Gloria. Tomorrow is March seventh.

GLORIA   It isn't Christmas?

Anthony reaches into his pocket. He produces a slim, shiny wrapped gift.

ANTHONY   No. But I did get you a gift.

GLORIA   What is it?

ANTHONY   A way we can see anything we want. Or anyone. You can see Craig. You can see me. I can see you.

Anthony extends the shiny gift to Gloria. She takes it.

GLORIA   Seriously?

ANTHONY   Seriously, seriously.

The gift box in Gloria's hand beeps. It is the unmistakable tone of an iPhone activating "Siri." She drops it on the floor, with a start.

They both look at Anthony's gift.

GLORIA   ...What is that?

ANTHONY   Our own private island. Even if I'm not there, you can look at it and see me. And I can see you.

GLORIA   I need to see you. When I don't see you, I fall apart.

ANTHONY   So do I.

The shiny gift beeps. Anthony and Gloria look at each other.

END OF PLAY.

Christmas for New Year's
by Jennifer Reichert

CHARACTERS
MATT – male, late 20s, scruffy
ANDY – female, late 20s, punky

SETTING
A snowy Amtrak platform. Evening.

For permission to produce this play, please contact the playwright at:
jennifer@jenniferreichert.com

Lights rise on a snowy Amtrak platform. A small ticket office, adorned with colored Christmas lights, casts light onto the falling snow. MATT, late 20s, scruffy, wearing a thin coat and hospital scrubs, scrambles quickly onto the platform.

MATT   Andy? Andy!

Matt sprints down the platform, pulling out his phone. He dials, searching the windows of the train as he runs down the platform.

MATT   *(cont'd)* Andy! Pick up, pick up. No-no-no!

The sounds of the train releasing its brake and pulling out of the station. Matt lurches to a halt.

Behind him, ANDY, a girl in her 20s, bundled up, drags her wheelie suitcase from the ticket office.

ANDY   Matt?

Matt turns and sees her. He runs to her and picks her up in his arms, spinning her around.

MATT   You stayed.

ANDY   Put me down!

Matt sets her down.

MATT   I thought I missed you. When it pulled out...

ANDY   That's the train to Portland. My train isn't for another five minutes.

MATT   Oh.

ANDY   What are you doing here?

MATT   You're really going to LA?

ANDY Yes. You got my message.

MATT We had plans. You can't just cancel our Christmas plans.

ANDY We were only going to hang out for a few hours, Matt. And it seemed like you might not be able to anyway... I was talking to Mike, and he asked me to come for the week.

MATT You haven't seen that guy in years.

ANDY Yeah, I've been here. He's a good friend. And he's free.

MATT Because he doesn't have a job. You'll be on the train on Christmas Eve. On Christmas. When are you coming back?

ANDY The third.

MATT You'll be there for New Year's.

ANDY You cancelled New Year's. Mike has a gig then. I've missed him. And since I didn't have anything else going on—

MATT But you did. We had plans for Christmas.

ANDY We had plans for Thanksgiving, too. And I ate a turkey by myself. And you barely asked me to come over for Christmas. That's not plans.

MATT That's not true.

ANDY And you had New Year's Eve.

MATT I thought I explained—

ANDY In a forty second voice mail this morning.

MATT I just found out this morning.

ANDY A *backdoor* voicemail–

MATT I said I was sorry. What's your problem?

ANDY I bought a dress, Matt. If you didn't notice, I don't wear dresses. But I bought a dress. A smokin', back cut down to nothing, black, sparkly, thigh slit dress. But you took an extra shift, jerk.

MATT So wear it to Mike's gig!

ANDY I wanted to see your face when you saw me in it. You're an asshole.

MATT It was either New Year's or Christmas–

The sounds of a train approaching. Andy checks the time.

ANDY Well, Christmas doesn't have kissing. I thought if we were together for New Year's Eve, if I was in that dress... When midnight came, we'd be at that party where we don't know anybody, and you would look at me and say "Happy New Year!" And that's when I would kiss you, Matt. And in that dress, you would kiss me right back. If you saw me in that dress? Really saw me? Not just good ol' let's-watch-hockey-Andy, but frickin' sex-bomb-Andy-who-can't-be-denied. *(beat)* But you cancelled. You cancelled it. You were the reason I stayed in this town, when everyone else left, Matt. So now I'm going to LA. I don't know if I'm coming back.

The train has pulled into the station, hissing to a stop.

MATT Charney said I had to choose Christmas or New Year's. He's my boss, and I *had* to choose. Which day I was going to spend with you. For me Christmas is the day you spend with the people

MATT   *(cont'd)* you're close to. Or want to be close to. *(beat)* I made reservations. Three weeks ago. For the inn with the ducks. I got us tickets for the skating pond. As a surprise. So. I hoped this Christmas *would* have kissing. *(beat)* And now I screwed it up. It's all to hell.

Matt's beeper goes off. He silences it.

ANDY   How was I supposed to know that?

The train whistles. Andy checks the clock.

MATT   Please stay here with me.

ANDY   You're on shift?

MATT   Yeah. I stole an ambulance.

ANDY   Matt!

MATT   I'm kidding. But I'm not supposed to be here.

ANDY   You need to get back to the hospital.

MATT   I will.

The conductor calls "All Aboard!" OR The train whistles brashly.

MATT   That's your train.

Matt's beeper goes off. He silences it and shoves the beeper in his pocket. She looks at him. The train doors close, and the train hisses, releasing its brake. Matt looks back at her, just standing there.

MATT   *(cont'd)* You missed your train.

ANDY   Oops.

Andy drops her suitcase. She kisses him soundly.

MATT I thought you had a plan to kiss me on New Year's Eve.

ANDY Oops.

And he kisses her right back.

After a moment, they break the kiss. He picks up her suitcase. She takes his hand and they walk down the platform side by side.

ANDY *(cont'd)* Do you think they'd mind if I wore a slinky black dress to their Christmas inn?

MATT I don't give a damn if they mind or not. Festive is festive.

They walk off into the snowy night.

END OF PLAY.

Winter Break
by Kitt Lavoie

CHARACTERS
JACKSON – male, 19
JESSICA – female, 20

SETTING
A crowded Amtrak train approaching New York's Penn Station

For permission to produce this play, please contact the playwright at:
kitt@kittlavoie.com

Lights rise on a crowded Amtrak train. JACKSON, 19, and JESSICA, 20, sit crammed into seats across from each other, their backpacks and luggage in a mountain around them. Jackson stares out the icy windows, cozy in a Drexel University sweatshirt. Jessica watches him. After a moment, a nearby speaker crackles:

CONDUCTOR *(over loudspeaker)* Penn Station, next stop. Next stop, New York Penn Station.

Jessica looks at Jackson. She breathes deep.

JESSICA Just do it, Jack.

JACKSON I'm not going to.

JESSICA Christmas is for family, Jackson.

JACKSON I know. And that's why I'm spending it with you.

Jackson smiles at Jessica. They look at each other a moment. Jackson turns back to the window. They chug along. After a moment, Jessica unzips her knapsack and pulls out a small wrapped box. She reaches over and places it on Jackson's lap. He looks down at the box, then up at Jessica.

JESSICA It's a present.

Jackson grins and begins to pull back the corner of the wrapping.

JESSICA *(cont'd)* It's from your mom.

Jackson stops. He looks up at Jessica.

JACKSON What are you doing talking to her?

JESSICA She called me. When you weren't answering.

JACKSON That's between me and her.

JESSICA It's between me, too. She wants to see you, Jack.

Jackson shakes his head. He hands the unopened box back to Jessica and turns to look out the window. She watches him a moment, then tears the wrapping off the box and puts it back in Jackson's lap.

JESSICA (cont'd) Open it.

Jackson flips open the top of the box. He looks inside. He looks away, a little more moved by the contents of the box than he wants to be.

JESSICA (cont'd) What is it?

Jackson reaches into the box and pulls out...

JACKSON Socks.

He separates the socks and pulls one over each forearm, making little hand puppets that talk wordlessly at each other. He balls up his fists, rubbing them on his forehead.

JACKSON (cont'd) It's always socks.

JESSICA She wants to see you, Jack. Call her.

Jessica reaches into her bag and pulls out her cell phone. She offers it out to Jackson.

JACKSON I can't.

JESSICA Jack—

Jackson holds up his socked hands.

JACKSON No fingers.

Jackson pulls the socks off his hands and tosses them to lay limply on Jessica's backpack. Jessica looks at them, then to Jackson.

JESSICA You need to get off, Jackson.

JACKSON	Jess–
JESSICA	My parents don't know you're coming.
JACKSON	Why?
JESSICA	Because you're not.

Jackson looks at her, flummoxed.

JESSICA	(cont'd) We've spent the past three months. I can't spend Christmas pretending. I can't sit there in my slippers and my pancakes Christmas morning and pretend. This isn't working anymore, Jack.
JACKSON	So... you got me on this train so you could tell me here? So I would have to get off and go back to school? And spend Christmas alone?
JESSICA	No, I got you on this train because I think you should go home. And I think you're as stubborn as you are smart, and you hate to be alone. They're fifteen blocks away, Jack. Don't be stupid.
JACKSON	I'm not stupid.
JESSICA	About this, you are.
JACKSON	You invited me to your *house*.
JESSICA	I *didn't* invite you. You invited you. And I'm sorry if you think I'm all you've got anymore, but you did that, not me. And I can't spend any more time feeling like you continue to entertain the idea of me just because I'm the only one left.
JACKSON	Do you know what I gave up to be with you? You want to talk about stupid?

JESSICA	I know what you gave up. And what I'm saying is, go get those things back.

The brakes of the train squeal.

CONDUCTOR *(over the loudspeaker)* New York Penn Station. Station stop New York.

The brakes hiss, and the doors of the train clatter open. The sound of passengers gathering their things. Jackson does not move.

JACKSON	I don't "entertain the idea of you." Don't say that. It's Christmas. I know I haven't been always fair. Over the past few months. But the time of year... it makes things clear. You know?

JESSICA	I know.

JACKSON	And I'm saying, I want to watch you eat pancakes on Christmas morning.

JESSICA	And I'm saying I think you should go home.

JACKSON	I'm trying to say I'm sorry.

JESSICA	That might have made a difference in October. It really might have. But it's too late, Jack.

JACKSON	*It's never too late.*

JESSICA	*Then go home.* I didn't ask you to give them up for me. And it's making you awful, you miss them so much.

CONDUCTOR *(over the loudspeaker)* All aboard! Next stop, Yonkers!

Jackson looks at Jessica. Their eyes are locked.

JACKSON	I don't miss them.

JESSICA		It's making *us* awful. And I can't do that anymore.
JACKSON		So that's it?
JESSICA		I don't know. Maybe.
JACKSON		So just, "Merry Christmas. Get off my train"?
JESSICA		Not just "get off my train." I'm saying *go home*. I'm saying stop punishing *her* for what *he* did. Stop punishing *him*. *It's Christmas,* Jack.

A beat.

JACKSON		You didn't even get me a gift, did you?
JESSICA		I got you the ticket, Jack.

Jessica takes the strewn socks off her bag and holds them out to Jackson.

JESSICA		*(cont'd)* Now... Merry Christmas.
JACKSON		"...but get off my train?"

Jessica can't quite look at him. But she nods gently. Jackson rises. He looks down on Jessica.

JACKSON		I'm just going to get the return train back to Philly. You understand?
JESSICA		I think he'd be sorry, Jack. If you'd let him.

Jackson eyes her, then hurriedly wrangles up his bags. He turns to Jessica.

JACKSON		Tell your folks Merry Christmas.

Jackson hustles off the train, leaving Jessica with the socks dangling limply from her hands. She looks at them, then folds them and tucks them gently into her backpack. She sits for a moment.

The train doors clunk shut. And the train begins to move.

Blackout.

END OF PLAY.

Counting the Days
by Cavan Hallman

CHARACTERS
JERRY – male, 50s, a brilliant interrogator precisely because he seems as friendly as your favorite uncle

YANN – male, late 20s, withered from being held far too long in a dark detention facility, non-native English speaker

SETTING
An unnamed American detention facility that is not in America

*For permission to produce this play, please contact the playwright at:
cavanhallman@gmail.com*

Darkness. We hear two deep raps against a steel door. We hear the door creak open, then slam shut. Lights rise and we see a small prison cell. JERRY, 50s, *stands just inside the cell door. He wears glasses, a short-sleeve button-up, and slacks, like a friendly mission controller at NASA. He holds a can of Coca-Cola in one hand and a brown paper bag in the other.* YANN, *late 20s, a very thin man in a prisoner's uniform, is on his knees, facing the wall, hands on head. He speaks English with a foreign accent.*

JERRY You can stand. How you doin' today?

YANN (*standing*) Fine, thank you.

JERRY That's all?

YANN Yes. Fine is actually quite good.

JERRY Sure. (*A long pause.*) This is for you.

He hands Yann the Coke. Yann opens it and guzzles. He takes a break, looks at Jerry, slightly puzzled. His eyes keep being drawn to the bag. Yann sucks down some soda. He looks at the bag again. Drawn to it, Yann takes a self-censored step forward.

JERRY (*cont'd*) That was a balk, buddy.

YANN Enough baseball. I think you made it all up.

JERRY It's a real thing. A beautiful thing, that game.

Yann's attention keeps shifting between Jerry and his bag.

YANN The rules are like how a crazy person thinks.

JERRY If it's real.

YANN Yes. If you told me the truth.

JERRY You wanna know what's in the bag. You keep looking at it.

YANN   No. I don't.

JERRY   You do.

YANN   I'm sorry.

JERRY   You're curious. It's alright to be curious.

YANN   No. It's not. I'm sorry. I won't look.

JERRY   Hey. Don't... I've been good to you. Right?

Yann nods affirmative.

YANN   Then you leave. And it doesn't ever stay good for too long.

JERRY   Well, I'm sorry about that. I'd stay if I could. I really would, little buddy.

YANN   I believe you.

Yann finishes the Coca-Cola in one final giant gulp.

JERRY   *(yelling off)* Guard!

A window slides open at the top of the cell door. A new can of Coke appears. Jerry takes it. The window closes.

JERRY   *(cont'd, off)* I'll trade ya!

The window opens. The empty can is removed and the window closes again.

JERRY   *(cont'd)* Go ahead. It's all yours.

Jerry hands the can to Yann, who opens it and begins drinking immediately. Another pause. Yann drinks again.

YANN   You don't want one?

JERRY	I'm up to my ears in that crap. Gotta leave room for some ham later. It's commissary ham, but it's ham. And I think they got those pineapple rings with the "mara-skeeno" cherries.
YANN	I don't know it.
JERRY	They're real good. *(beat)* I *want* you to want to see what's in the bag. I want you to be curious, to want to know things... to be a person.

Jerry takes a gift-wrapped package out of the bag.

JERRY	*(cont'd)* Merry Christmas, Yann. It's Christmas Day. Thought I'd bring you something.
YANN	That is your holiday Jerry, not mine.
JERRY	A "holiday." I wish it was. Wish I was back home.
YANN	What month is this?
JERRY	December.
YANN	Christmas is always in December?
JERRY	Yeah.
YANN	Then this is still 2005?
JERRY	You got it.
YANN	That's good. I've been counting right.
JERRY	Gotta wake up pretty early to get something past you, huh, little buddy? *(beat)* Aren't ya gonna open the present? I wrapped it myself.
YANN	It's not my religion.

JERRY   It ain't a religious thing. Everybody in America celebrates Christmas. Growing up, a Jewish kid had the biggest tree on my block. Every year. A Jew. *(beat)* Okay, not the best example. Your people and their people have their differences, whatever... Christmas is for everyone. It's a gift. Open it.

They both stare at the package as Yann fails to open it.

JERRY   *(cont'd)* What's wrong?

YANN   Am I in America?

JERRY   No, but you're with us. That's the important part. You're helping us out, and I can't tell you how much I appreciate that.

YANN   You have more questions?

JERRY   I do, but not today. Today I'm here as a friend. It's Christmas. I wanted to show this to you. Open it. For me. As a friend. *(beat)* If I went to visit your house and you told me to take off my shoes before dinner I would do it and not even ask a second question about it. I'd be polite. Do you know how much I hate for people to see my feet? I hate it a lot. But I'd do it. I'd just do it. For you. Out of respect. And friendship.

Yann opens the wrapping, reluctantly.

JERRY   *(cont'd)* It's a baseball almanac. Now you know I'm not making it all up. There's no way I could just whip up something like this. *(beat)* The Yankees are a real thing. Baseball. All of it. Take a look.

Yann flips through the pages, book in lap, sipping his Coca-Cola.

YANN   You *could*. You could make something like this.

JERRY But I'm not that bored. Look. Look up anything you want. I used to get one of these for my boy every year. Good kid. But every kid's gotta rebel. Sometime. Somehow. So I get him this book and not a day later he can't stop talking about the Cincinnati Reds. Can't be bothered with the Yankees. No. Takes down every poster I put up for him. Won't stop talking about Frank Robinson and his slugging percentage, and Johnny Bench, and Joe Morgan – you ever heard that guy call a game? He's an idiot. The Cincinnati Reds. They won a Series with Barry Larkin and Rob Dibble. Nobodies. It's disgusting. Who remembers Jose Rijo? No one. And Donnie Baseball got bupkus? But at least my boy wasn't a Sox fan. And at least the Reds are NL'ers. And they ain't the Mets. Amirite?

YANN Jerry, something is strange here. It says the Babe played for the Red Sox. Is that true?

JERRY It is.

YANN And he was a pitcher?

JERRY Yeah, that too.

YANN A very good pitcher.

JERRY It's all true. He was Hall of Fame quality, then those bean-faces sold him for pennies on the dollar – cheap – and didn't win another Series for about a million years.

YANN You said they won last year.

JERRY They did. Good for them. Real good for them. It's cute they finally got one.

YANN This is for me? Really?

JERRY Yeah. *(beat)* Kind of. *(beat)* I can't leave it with you, of course.

YANN Right. Of course.

JERRY But you can look at it for as long as I'm here.

YANN Okay.

Yann turns through several more pages of the Baseball Almanac. He finishes his second can of Coke.

YANN *(cont'd)* Will you be staying long?

JERRY *(yelling off)* Guard! Two!

The little window opens and Jerry receives two more cans of soda. He gives one to Yann.

YANN We could talk.

JERRY Go ahead and check out the book, little buddy. I got nowhere special to be. Except for that ham and pineapple.

Yann quietly scans a couple pages. Jerry watches, satisfied.

YANN I think I can tell what the abbreviations mean.

JERRY Well, let me know if you have any questions.

YANN You taught me the game very well.

Yann becomes emotional, suddenly overwhelmed.

YANN *(cont'd)* I understand it all. Thank you.

JERRY You're welcome.

YANN Christmas, Jerry. Merry to Christmas.

Jerry cracks open his Coke and watches as Yann continues to absorb the statistics. The lights fade to black.

END OF PLAY.

Little One
by Julia Bilbao

CHARACTERS
LEILA – female, late 20s
TREVOR – male, late 20s

SETTING
A Brooklyn apartment, Christmas Eve, present day

For permission to produce this play, please contact the playwright at:
julbilbao@gmail.com

Brooklyn, NY. Present Day. A twinkly Christmas tree sits in the corner of an apartment living area. LEILA, late 20s, kneels at the foot of the tree gazing up at it. In the adjoining kitchen a nearly empty bottle of red wine sits on the counter. Keys jingle, as a door is unlocked. TREVOR, late 20s, enters. His wool coat is sprinkled with snow. He stomps his boots off and throws them aside. He heaves a grocery bag onto the counter.

TREVOR   Ho ho ho hot chocolate and George Bailey's!

Trevor sees the wine.

TREVOR   *(cont'd)* Wow – I see you've gotten started without me.

Leila holds her face in her hands and begins to weep.

TREVOR   *(cont'd)* Uh oh…

Leila turns her face to him. Tears mixed with mascara stream down her face.

LEILA   I can't believe he's gone…

She bursts into sobs and runs to him.

TREVOR   Oh God… but your uncle's lab results were optimistic last week. When did this happen? Why didn't you call me?

LEILA   It was so sudden…

TREVOR   I'm so sorry Leila. But he was 76 – he had a long life.

LEILA   He was my furry little muffin!

TREVOR   Wait what?

LEILA   Rest in peace, Pierre. I will never forget you.

TREVOR   Your hamster?

LEILA   Gerbil! He's a gerbil! *Was* a gerbil... was...

TREVOR   Alright, we need to remember to breathe, right?

Leila nods and sniffles as she slows her breathing. She closes her eyes and begins taking slow, long breaths. In through the nose, out through the mouth. Trevor begins pulling ingredients out of the grocery bag and puts a saucepan on the stove.

TREVOR   *(cont'd)* What *you* need is some hot chocolate. I got the good stuff! Dark chocolate Godiva and *real* marshmallows. Not the chalky little mouse turds that come in the packet...

LEILA   His little turds... I'm going to miss his little turds.

Trevor abandons the hot chocolate and guides Leila to a stool at the kitchen counter. She sits. He takes the stool next to her.

TREVOR   Breathe. ...Want to tell me what happened?

LEILA   Something horrible.

TREVOR   Just keep breathing.

LEILA   So his Christmas present was delivered today and I just couldn't wait to give it to him till tomorrow...

TREVOR   That ball that they run around in, right?

LEILA   Yes, but the best one there is. The Kritter Krawler 3000. I put it in his cage and it was so cute– he jumped right in! But there just wasn't enough room in there for him to run around without banging into things so... I brought him out to the hallway.

TREVOR   Oh no...

LEILA   He was surprisingly very good at it and well... he found the stairs.

TREVOR   Jesus.

LEILA   I think he broke his neck. He made this little squeak and it echoed in the stairwell... I can't stop hearing it.

TREVOR   It's going to be okay... what did you do with him?

LEILA   Well... when you got here I was in the middle of saying goodbye...

Leila wipes away her tears, walking towards the Christmas tree. Trevor follows.

LEILA   *(cont'd)* I will never forget you, Pierre. You will always be in my heart.

Hanging next to a football-playing Santa Claus ornament is a transparent plastic ball. The Kritter Krawler 3000... and Pierre is still inside it.

TREVOR   That is... unsanitary.

LEILA   I know.

TREVOR   Why'd you hang him on the tree?

LEILA   I don't really know. But I'm having trouble taking him down.

TREVOR   Okay well my family is coming tomorrow, Leila.

LEILA   I know.

Trevor cautiously reaches for the ornament.

TREVOR   Why don't we move him to–

LEILA   No! Don't touch him!

TREVOR   Why are you being weird about this?

LEILA   I just *murdered* my gerbil, Trevor.

TREVOR   You didn't *murder* him. You just... facilitated his death.

LEILA   Exactly. If it weren't for me, he'd be alive.

TREVOR   Not necessarily. You probably gave him a longer life than normal. He could have been eaten by a family dog or strangled by an overly lovable toddler... or fed to the snakes at the pet store.

LEILA   Great so I'm an *overly lovable* murderer.

TREVOR   It was an accident, Leila.

LEILA   It being an accident doesn't excuse anything. Lives are lost out of negligence all the time. Children or elderly people have been left in cars on 100-degree days with the windows closed...

TREVOR   *(joking)* Would you like to file a wrongful death claim against yourself? The courthouse is definitely closed tomorrow but we can be there first thing Monday morning.

LEILA   Why do you have to make light of *everything*, Trevor? I'm *upset*.

TREVOR   I'm really sorry your gerbil died, Leila. You need to forgive yourself though.

LEILA   I don't know how.

TREVOR   Well, hanging him on the Christmas tree definitely isn't the solution. He deserves a proper burial, right? Let's take him to the park.

LEILA   The ground is frozen.

TREVOR   You don't know that for sure—

LEILA   I already tried.

Leila collapses onto the couch. Trevor joins her.

TREVOR   I'm sorry this happened. But do you really want Charlie here tomorrow with Pierre hanging up there in plain sight? He's a toddler; you know how curious he is. He puts everything he can get his hands on in his mouth.

LEILA   I got Charlie's present today.

TREVOR   Hey, that's great! Did you go to that place that just opened on North 4th?

LEILA   It's called Wee Babe. Yeah.

TREVOR   What'd you end up getting?

LEILA   An interactive lamb stuffed animal named Liz. There was an interactive donkey named Don too and I was trying to decide if I should get him the boy animal or the girl animal and I decided that I shouldn't have to get him the dumb male donkey toy just because he's a boy.

TREVOR   True. I'm sure he'll love it.

LEILA   *(suddenly)* I would've been due next week, Trevor.

A beat. Trevor puts his arm around her.

TREVOR   You did the right thing.

LEILA   I know.

TREVOR   You—

LEILA	Have three more years of med school. I know.
TREVOR	And by the time you're done you'll be thirty-two. And we can actually plan for it. I could use those three years to get my savings in a good place too.
LEILA	I know.

Leila picks herself up and approaches the tree. Trevor follows. She gently takes the Kritter Krawler down and makes her way to the kitchen. She holds the plastic ball out to Trevor.

LEILA	*(cont'd)* Will you open it please?

Trevor takes the ball in his hands and opens it. Leila carefully scoops Pierre out.

LEILA	*(cont'd)* Merry Christmas, little one. I'm going to put you in the garbage can outside now... I'm so sorry.
TREVOR	I could call someone. See if we can get a hole dug–
LEILA	That's all right. I'll say goodbye to him out there.

Leila puts Pierre inside an empty grocery bag, slips on her shoes, and grabs her coat.

LEILA	*(cont'd)* I'll be right back.
TREVOR	Ok.

Leila exits leaving Trevor. He looks down at Pierre's Christmas present in his hands. He fiddles with it for a moment until it's back in one piece. Then, taking it by the string, he hangs it back up on the tree. Blackout.

END OF PLAY.

Hot Air
by Katelin Wilcox

CHARACTERS
CHARLIE – any gender/age/ethnicity, a giant elf balloon, cranky
KIT – any gender/age/ethnicity, a giant elf balloon, cheerful
CJ – any gender/age/ethnicity, a giant elf balloon, fatalistic

SETTING
The Macy's Thanksgiving Day Parade balloon storage area, the night before Thanksgiving

For permission to produce this play, please contact the playwright at:
katelinwilcox@hotmail.com

Lights up on KIT, CHARLIE, and CJ. They are the giant vintage elf balloons that have preceded the Santa Claus float in the Macy's Thanksgiving Day Parade since 1947.

Charlie sits grumpily, massaging one knee. Kit is cheerfully doing stretches and physical warm ups. CJ sits quietly in a corner, face ashen.

CHARLIE Ugh, my legs are stiff.

KIT *(taking a deep breath, continuing to stretch)* Just wait til tomorrow. Once you're fully inflated and floating the friendly skies again you'll feel much better.

CHARLIE Well, until then, I'm stiff.

KIT You say that *every year*.

CHARLIE *Excuuuse me.* What would you like to talk about? *(beat) Lampposts?*

Kit shoots Charlie a sharp look and checks to see if CJ heard the comment.

KIT *(whispers)* Not. Cool.

CHARLIE Hey, CJ! Hey. Buddy. Look, I know it's not the best news. How ya doing?

CJ *(suddenly exploding)* HOW DO YOU THINK?!?!

KIT Okay, okay, calm down.

CJ Calm down? Tomorrow morning, my life is going to be in the slippery little hands of the worst balloon handler Macy's has ever seen!

KIT She's... fine!

CJ She's not fine! The texting. The Facebooking. The Instagramming! Last year, Miss "Cell Phone Susie" went one-handed for six blocks, and there was a

CJ	*(cont'd)* distinct whiff of spiked eggnog on her breath! SpongeBob was behind her the whole time and saw her weaving all over Herald Square. He was disgusted.
KIT	Okay, but nothing happened, right?
CJ	That's because she was on Spiderman and Spiderman's got 91 handlers! She's worked at Macy's for what – five minutes? These whippersnappers have no idea what it takes to be a handler. CONSTANT VIGILANCE! One distracted moment and it's *right into a lamppost* for us! Old Man Wozniak – now HE was a handler. Got me through the Great Gust of '83. What do you think would have happened to me if Cell Phone Susie had been at the reins?
CHARLIE	Settle down drama queen. You've been in storage too long. We've each got 12 handlers. It's not Spidey level, but one delinquent pair of hands isn't the end of the world.
CJ	You naïve little fool.
KIT	CJ!
CHARLIE	What did you call me?

Charlie rushes CJ, CJ hides behind Kit.

CJ	You won't look so tough tomorrow. The cushy days of 12 handlers are over. We've been downsized. Four each.
CHARLIE	*(retreating)* Where did you hear that?
CJ	Snoopy got his hands on a copy of this year's parade handbook. And you can bet he had a good laugh.

CHARLIE   *(re: Snoopy)* Smug jerk.

CJ   We're not videogame characters or from a Pixar movie. We're irrelevant. Nobody cares about us.

KIT   CJ! How can you say that?! We're not irrelevant. People love us!

CJ   Who? No one knows our names. No one even knows we HAVE names!

KIT   Look, I know we may not be the "hippest" balloons on the block, but we're part of something bigger than that. We're a nostalgic, Christmassy reminder of the coming of Santa Claus. We are heralds of the season.

CHARLIE   *(beat, quietly)* Give it a rest, Kit.

CJ   Face it. Tomorrow morning, we're going to be left to the mercy of a few teeny-boppers who are more interested in taking selfies than watching where they're going. Well, I'm not going to take it lying down.

KIT   What do you mean...?

CJ   I mean tomorrow morning when we round the corner of 7th Avenue and Central Park South – I'm breakin' loose.

Kit gasps.

KIT   C – J – Elf. No balloon has ever gone rogue like that. You would violate the code of our very existence and bring shame on this whole family.

CJ   Look, Little Miss Sunshine, since 1947 we've done things your way but you know what – they'll just have to find someone else to "herald the season."

KIT But – what'll happen to you?! Who knows where you could end up!

CJ At least it will be on my terms. And it'll be a hell of a ride.

CHARLIE Nobody's going for "a hell of a ride." You're staying right here with us. Jesus, pull it together. Worst case scenario, you get a little snagged, they patch you up.

CJ Tell that to Kermit. He's never been the same since he took that lamppost to the gut. He's always drifting to the left! *(quieter)* And public humiliation aside, you and I both know that a patch job is not the "worst case scenario."

Charlie tries to shush CJ.

KIT What are you talking about?

CHARLIE Nothing.

CJ I'm talking about PERMANENT STORAGE.

KIT That's... a myth. A spook story they tell new balloons to keep them in line.

CJ It's no myth. What do you think happens to balloons that are too damaged to repair? Send them off to... live with some relatives on a farm in the country?? Cat in the Hat. Bullwinkle. Jesus, BARNEY! Stabbed and stomped down like a rabid dog. That parade route is *littered* with corpses of good balloons taken down by lampposts at the hands of negligent handlers.

Kit is aghast.

CHARLIE That's enough!

Charlie starts toward CJ.

CJ: Bring it! I dare you. I am an angry elf balloon and I've got nothing to lose!

Charlie stops. Beat.

CHARLIE: Of course you do. We all do. Did you ever stop to think WHY "Cell Phone Susie" took all those selfies?

CJ: Because she's a product of a media-saturated, self-obsessed generation?!

CHARLIE: Yes. But also - because she was doing something worth posting about.

CJ: Because she was on Spiderman.

CHARLIE: And do you know why she's NOT on Spiderman this year?

CJ: Probably got demoted. Too many mistakes, so they stuck her on a balloon nobody cared about.

CHARLIE: She ASKED to get switched to you.

A beat.

CJ: Why?

CHARLIE: "Cell Phone Susie's" last name happens to be Wozniak.

CJ: As in...

CHARLIE: As in Old Man Wozniak's daughter.

CJ: *(flustered)* Well – clearly balloon handling skill does NOT run in the family.

CHARLIE	Will you give it a rest. Wozniak Senior's not doing too well this year. And if her dad's going to have to watch the parade from a hospital bed, *Susan* wants him to see her walking under the same balloon he handled for 40 years.
KIT	How do you know that?
CHARLIE	CJ's not the only one with sources. Spidey can't keep his mouth shut. *(beat)* So. Whether it's "heralding the season," or putting a smile on a sick old man's face, or – so help me – catching a glimpse of Betty Boop bouncing down 7th Avenue, we've all got skin in this game.

A beat.

KIT	Really? Betty?
CHARLIE	Don't judge me. I hate to see her leave, but I love to watch her go.
CJ	Betty's not in the parade this year.
CHARLIE	I know that. And you don't see *me* flying the coop.

A beat.

CJ	I guess... I could give Cell Ph- uh, *Susan* the... benefit of the doubt–
KIT	Really?
CJ	But I'm not doing it for her! I'm doing it for him. After 40 years, I owe him that.
CHARLIE	*(sarcastically)* Well, that's the spirit.
KIT	And she's gonna post sooo many pictures of you... *(off CJ's wary look)* uh, after – AFTER! – the parade.

KIT	*(cont'd)* So much for being "irrelevant"! Who's irrelevant now?!
CHARLIE	Pikachu*. *(beat)* Seriously. Why is he still a balloon?!
KIT	It's... okay Charlie. I'm sure they'll bring Betty back soon.

Kit pats Charlie on the shoulder.

KIT	*(cont'd)* In the meantime, *(Kit smiles)* we've got a big day tomorrow...

Kit starts doing the stretches and physical warm ups again, encouraging the others to join. Deep breathing. Calisthenics. Charlie and CJ reluctantly join Kit, rolling their eyes at first, then with more gusto. Lights fade.

END OF PLAY.

---

* Productions should feel free to substitute whatever seems like the least-relevant balloon in that year's parade

Playwright Biographies

Julia Bilbao (*Anniephylaxis, Little One*) has been involved with The CRY HAVOC Company since 2011. Her other Very Short Holiday Plays include *Sanctuary, Gracie,* and *Fire+Ice*. She graduated from Skidmore College with a BS in Theater and works in the New York entertainment industry as a scenic artist.

Mélisa Breiner-Sanders (*Year After Year*) is a writer, producer and actor living in Queens, NY. Her writing projects include *Year After Year, Him&Her&Him* (short film), and *We're Breaking Up* (Web Series). As a producer Mélisa has worked on a variety of projects including the feature film *Seven Lovers* (Available on Amazon and iTunes), *Being Here, Him&Her&Him, Believin', My Secret Friend* and many more. MFA in Acting from DePaul University, proud member of SAG-AFTRA and Actors Equity Association, and Resident Artist with The CRY HAVOC Company. For more information visit BreinerSandersProductions.com and MelisaBS.com

Annalisa Chamberlin (*Involuntary Counsel*) is an actor who also writes plays and music, plays music, and sings. She is a Resident Artist at The CRY HAVOC Company where she has developed several short plays and has appeared in numerous company productions and workshops. She attended the New York Conservatory for Dramatic Arts (NYCDA) and has continued to live in the city, working on various creative collaborations in writing, composing, and acting in independent films, theater and musical theater. She has appeared in the New York Musical Festival (NYMF) twice (2015 and 2019), and she has performed in a variety of theaters and venues in Manhattan, including the Irish Arts Center, The Cell Theater, HERE Arts Center, IRT Theater, New York Theater Workshop's 4th Street Theater, and Hudson Guild Theater. Annalisa will be forever grateful to the public school teachers and the public school arts programs that she was so lucky to have early on. And for her incredible parents who were the first artists she ever looked up to, and the first to believe in her.

Will Clark (*IRL*) Originally hailing from South Eastern Connecticut, Will is a New York-based film and theater actor. Will is a Resident Artist and Associate Artistic Director of The CRY

HAVOC Company. With CRY HAVOC, Will has taken part in the development of over 150 new plays, musicals, and screenplays, and has performed in dozens of CRY HAVOC's readings and productions, including his performance in *Sabbatical* for the Lincoln Center Originals series. With CRY HAVOC, Will has developed other short plays he has written including *Color Blind*, *Carry Me On*, *Unverdant Beauty*, and *Crimson and Closure*. Will has also directed workshop productions of *Then...* by Cynthia Franks, *Michael Bay's America: Part IV* by Jerzy Gwiazdowski, and *The Earth You Created* by Sydney Painter. Other acting credits include *Cabaret* (Ivoryton Playhouse), *The Fantasticks* (Ivoryton Playhouse), *Three Sisters* (Gowanus Arts), *realer than that* (CRY HAVOC), *Wish You Were Here*, *My Love* (Planet Connections Festival), *Ectospasms* (New York Fringe), *The Most Interesting Man in Dave's Mind* (Samuel French OOB Festival), *AVoid2Remembr* (Interrobang Festival), and a residency with the FSGA Commedia Company.

Sharon E. Cooper (*Believin'*, *The Seven Men of Hanukkah*) is an award-winning, internationally produced and published playwright living in New York City. Her short plays have had productions in Singapore, The Netherlands, Germany, England, Hungary, India, Australia, and across the United States. She is published in *The Best 10-Minute Plays: 2010, 2014* and *2016*; *Laugh Lines: Short Comic Plays*; *The Bedford Introduction to Literature* and many other college textbooks. With Daryl Lathon, Sharon started Coopathon Productions where they adapted her CRY HAVOC-developed plays *The Seven Men of Hanukkah* and *Believin'* into short films. *The Seven Men of Hanukkah* screened on the festival circuit around the country, was a winner of the Boston Jewish Film Festival and was distributed in North America and South Asia on DIRECTV. Her feature length romantic comedy screenplay *The Golden Age of Kali* was a Second Rounder in the Austin Film Festival, a Quarter Finalist in the PAGE Awards and a Black List reviewer wrote that the she "characterizes Indian family culture with rich authenticity, specificity, vividness and joy." Sharon is a yoga instructor and a writing coach. She would like to thank The CRY HAVOC Company for their continued support and for making her a better writer. www.sharonecooper.com IG: @sharonecoop

Jennifer Curfman (*Anyway*) is a New York City-based director, actor, and co-Artistic Director of The CRY HAVOC Company. As a director and associate director, Jennifer's credits include: The Public Theater, Lincoln Center Originals, Pioneer Theatre, New York Shakespeare Exchange, Stagedoor Manor, Vital Theater, FringeNYC/Encores, Live from Lincoln Center, Joe's Pub, and Primary Stages. She has been seen onstage throughout the United States, with companies including the Shakespeare Theater of New Jersey, Great Lakes Theater Festival, and NYC Opera. She has taught acting, directing, and Shakespeare with The Public Theater (Hunts Point Children's Shakespeare Ensemble), NSKI Høyskole (Oslo, Norway), Stagedoor Studios, and the New School for Drama. Jennifer is a 2017 SDCF Observership Fellow, a member of the Lincoln Center Directors Lab and Actors' Equity Association, and an Associate Member of the Stage Directors and Choreographers Society. She holds a BFA from NYU.

Jim Fagan (*Black Sleigh Down, or White Christmas in Machu Picchu*) is a producer and director for Comedy Central and directed his first film, *Zero Issue*, with New York Picture Company. His play *Love Always: A Comedy on the pains of a life of love* is published by playscripts. He is a happy father and husband, unhappy Giants fan, is a proud alumni of many, many schools with many, many letters (BC/ASDS/UCB) and is considered to be too tall by more than some.

Jerzy Gwiazdowski (*Repeat, Repeat, Isle of View*) is an actor, playwright, and teacher based in NYC. Full-length plays include: *We Three* (LCI, Lincoln Center Directors Lab), *Proximity* (Sonnet Rep), *Lacy Hoodoo* (MUDasMAN), Short plays include: *Michael Bay's America, Part IV, All Over Me (How Does it Feel?), Vega, Two Birds* (CRY HAVOC). In November 2012, his short play *All Over Me* premiered simultaneously in Norway, Germany, and Australia. In 2015, he co-adapted *Take One Step* with original author Gerald Freedman for the 50th Anniversary of that musical's premiere production at Joseph Papp's New York Shakespeare Festival. Also in 2015, his short play *Grievous Circle* became the first play ever performed in the Rubinstein Atrium at Lincoln Center as part of *Lincoln Center Originals: The CRY HAVOC Company*. As an actor, he has appeared on Broadway, at regional theaters across the US, and in various television shows and feature films. Jerzy has served on the faculty of The New School for Drama (NYC) and as a guest instructor at NSKI Høyskole (Norwegian Actors College – Oslo, Norway). Studied at the UNC

School of the Arts. CRY HAVOC Resident Artist since 2010. Eight-time winner at the World Pun Championships.

Cavan Hallman (*Counting the Days*) Cavan's writing has been performed in NYC, New Orleans, Chicago, Ireland, on screen, and on tour. His touring plays, which he also directs, have been performed over 20,000 times for nearly 5 million students across the United States. He wrote the libretto and directed the world premiere of the musical *Pictures of Marilyn* at the National WWII Museum, named one of the ten best musicals of 2016 by *The New Orleans Times-Picayune*. He has also written commissioned pieces for the National Czech & Slovak Museum and KAPOOT Clown Theatre. Cavan is the founding Artistic Director of Mirrorbox Theatre, where he has directed the Iowa premieres of *Exit Strategy*, *Red Speedo*, *Luna Gale*, *There Is A Happiness That Morning Is*, among others. He serves as a new play development consultant and has taught and directed at Theatre Cedar Rapids. Cavan received his Bachelors' in Theatre from Columbia College Chicago and an MFA in Playwriting from the University of New Orleans, for whom he has also taught writing and acting, both on campus and for their study abroad program in Ireland. Cavan is a Resident Artist with The CRY HAVOC Company.

Ali Keller (*Dear Nate*) is a producer, dramaturg, and playwright committed to telling stories with complex female characters. She received her B.A. in Theatre Arts at Bucknell University. She is a Resident Playwright at The CRY HAVOC Company and a producer with the New York Picture Company and Bomb Girl Media (which she co-founded). Selected writing credits: *Standards* (The Dramatists Guild), *For Goodness Sake* (4th Street Theatre @ New York Theatre Workshop), *The Interview* (The Flea Serials – Cycle 43), and *Good For You* (Second Rounder at the 2018 Austin Film Festival Play Competition). Selected Film Credits: *Best Worst Thing That Ever Could Have Happened* (Production Assistant), *Zero Issue* (Producer), and *Seven Fishes* (Writer/Producer). Selected Associate/Assistant Director credits: *Lady Day at Emerson's Bar and Grill* (Broadway), *Live From Lincoln Center: Sweeney Todd*, and *Summit* (La Mama Experimental Theatre Club). Ali is a dramaturg with the New York Musical Festival (NYMF) where she worked with *PETER, WHO?*, which won Best Book in 2018. The song cycle she developed (*The F*ck Am I Doing?*)

in Adam Gwon's classes at ESPA appeared in the 2019 NYMF Concert Series. She is a Member of Stillwater Writers Group and a Member of the Dramatists Guild of America.

Kitt Lavoie (*And it came to pass in those days..., Fine, Winter Break*) is a director, playwright, and filmmaker – and is the only playwright ever to have their work performed on all seven continents during their lifetime. Plays and musical books include *Sabbatical* (Lincoln Center), *Kiki Baby* (Theater for the American Musical Prize), *The Median Line* (Herbert J. Robinson Award for Dramatic Writing), *realer than that* (winner, Samuel French New Play Festival), *And it came to pass in those days...* (Collective Press), *Good Enough* (Vintage Press), and *Bank & Trust* (Vintage Press). He wrote and produced the acclaimed feature-length documentary *Best Worst Thing That Ever Could Have Happened*, about the cast of the legendarily short-lived original Broadway production of Stephen Sondheim's *Merrily We Roll Along* (*New York Times*' Top 10 Films of 2016, *Newsweek*'s Favorite Documentaries of 2016, *Slate*'s Best Films of 2016, *The Wrap*'s Best Films of 2016, *Esquire*'s 20 Best Documentaries of All Time). Also a director, Kitt has staged more than 150 shows in the United States, Europe, and Asia. Kitt served for 22 years as the Founding Artistic Director of The CRY HAVOC Company. He is a member of the Stage Directors and Choreographers Society, the Dramatists Guild, and the Literary Managers and Dramaturgs of the Americas. www.kittlavoie.com

Sydney Painter (*On the Edge of What Might Happen*) has a BA in Theater Directing from Fordham University and is currently pursuing an MFA in Writing and Producing for Television from Loyola Marymount University in Los Angeles. She is originally from the San Francisco Bay Area where she directed many plays, most of them starring children, before she was swallowed by the grad school monster. She does not match her socks or do anything Marie Kondo says to do. Her favorite Beatle is George and her favorite Spice Girl is Ginger.

Jennifer Reichert (*Christmas for New Year's, Effigy, Snow Ball*) is a playwright, actor, and producer. Her play *Yukon Brass*, developed in the CRY HAVOC Workshop, was a semi-finalist in the Riant Strawberry One-Act Festival. Her plays have been performed all over the United States, as well as Canada, Colombia, and Norway. Other works include *Just Julian, Techs, Mikey Wears Braces, Intelligence,* and *Bake Sale.* Jennifer is a member of the Professional Playwrights Workshop at The Players, a Member of the Dramatists Guild, and a Resident Artist at The CRY HAVOC Company.

Katelin Wilcox (*Empty Handed, Ex-Mas, Hot Air*) is an actor and a playwright based in New York City. She has appeared in eight productions at the Shakespeare Theatre of New Jersey including *Pride and Prejudice, Cymbeline,* and *Comedy of Errors.* Other favorite acting credits include *Out of Tune* (Lincoln Center Originals), *Doubt* (Public Theatre of Maine), *Comedy of Errors* (Vermont Shakespeare Company), *Island* and *King John* (New York Shakespeare Exchange), and *realer than that* (The CRY HAVOC Company) – an award-winning play that has been adapted into a program to promote dialogue about sexual assault on college campuses. Katelin's one-woman show *The Pawnbroker*, which gives voice to the many women behind playwright Bertolt Brecht's body of work, had a critically-acclaimed run at FringeNYC and was extended as part of the Fringe Encore Series. Her work as a playwright has also been produced at the United Solo Festival (NYC), Lionheart Theatre Company (GA), Indiana Players (PA), Sandgate Theatre (Australia), Effulgent Productions (VA), and Ithaca College (NY). Katelin is a graduate of the University of Notre Dame, member of Actors Equity, Resident Artist with CRY HAVOC, partner-in-crime to Jeff, and mama to sweet Sylvia. www.katelinwilcox.com

Index of song and character inspirations from the Very Short Holiday Play writing assignment

As part of CRY HAVOC's annual Very Short Holiday Play assignment, each playwright was randomly assigned a song that was to, in some way, inspire the play, and were also asked to feature a character from another play that was developed in the CRY HAVOC Workshop.

Below are the songs and characters that inspired each of the plays in this collection.

A "family tree" showing the shared character connections between all of the plays from the first ten years of the annual Very Short Holiday Play collection is available at www.cryhavoccompany.org/familytree.

Snow Ball by Jennifer Reichert (2016)
   Inspiration song: "Foolish Games"
                     as performed by Jewel
   Character: Madison from her play *Just Julian*

Empty Handed by Katelin Wilcox (2016)
   Inspiration Song: "Together Again"
                     as performed by Janet Jackson
   Character: Joseph from her play *Last Call*

Black Sleigh Down, or White Christmas in Machu Picchu by Jim Fagan (2012)
   Inspiration song: "South America"
                     as performed by the Shout Out Louds
   Character: Leah from the play *Intelligence* by Jennifer Reichert

And it came to pass in those days... by Kitt Lavoie (2010)
   Inspiration song: "Here for You"
                     as performed by Neil Young
   Character: Cassie from his play *Makes Three*

The Seven Men of Hanukkah by Sharon E. Cooper (2013)
   Inspiration song: "What Good Am I?"
                     as performed by Tom Jones
   Character: Stephanie from her play *In the Mean Time*

Repeat, Repeat by Jerzy Gwiazdowski (2017)
Inspiration song: "Joy to the World"
as performed by the Mormon Tabernacle Choir
Character: Maureen and Gus from his play *All Over Me (How Does It Feel?)*

Anyway by Jennifer Curfman (2015)
Inspiration song: "I Would Be In Love (Anyway)"
as performed by Frank Sinatra
Character: Bennett from the play *Grievous Circle* by Jerzy Gwiazdowski

Anniephylaxis by Julia Bilbao (2015)
Inspiration song: "My Sweet Lady"
as performed by Frank Sinatra
Character: Annie from her play *See Ya Later, Alligator*

Dear Nate by Ali Keller (2013)
Inspiration song: "Make You Feel My Love"
as performed by Adele
Character: Cookie (Nate) from her play *Slut Claus*

Involuntary Counsel by Annalisa Chamberlin (2011)
Inspiration song: "Go Together"
as performed by Jillian Edwards
Character: Scott from the play *Not Entirely Platonic: Variations on a Confession* by Kitt Lavoie

Ex-Mas by Katelin Wilcox (2014)
Inspiration song: "Watching Movies"
as performed by Mac Miller
Character: Susan from her play *The Magic of Macy's*

Fine by Kitt Lavoie (2011)
Inspiration song: "Falling Apart Together"
as performed by Lee Brice
Character: Mel from his play *Bank & Trust*

On the Edge of What Might Happen by Sydney Painter (2014)
Inspiration song: "Keep Me Watching"
 as performed by Jason Walker
Character: Andy from the play *Ditch Pigs*
 by Emily Claire Schmidt

Effigy by Jennifer Reichert (2015)
Inspiration song: "Good Thing Going"
 as performed by Frank Sinatra
Character: Nadine from her play *Just Julian*

Year After Year by Mélisa Breiner-Sanders (2010)
Inspiration song: "Wish You Were Here"
 as performed by Pink Floyd
Character: Paul from her play *Lighthouse*

Believin' by Sharon E. Cooper (2014)
Inspiration song: "Watching You"
 as performed by Rodney Atkins
Character: Stephanie from her play *Occupied*

IRL by Will Clark (2011)
Inspiration song: "I Believe Jesus Brought Us Together"
 as performed by The Horrible Crowes
Character: Susan from his play *Eminent Domain*

Isle of View by Jerzy Gwiazdowski (2018)
Inspiration song: "1953"
 as performed by The National Parks
Character: Craig from his play
 All Over Me (How Does It Feel?)

Christmas for New Year's by Jennifer Reichert (2010)
Inspiration song: "Here Comes Your Man"
 as performed by Meaghan Smith
Character: Andy from her play *Mikey Wears Braces*

Winter Break by Kitt Lavoie (2009)
  Inspiration song: "Bring Them Home (If You Love Your Uncle Sam)"
           as performed by Pete Seeger, Billy Bragg,
           Ani Difranco, and Steve Earle
  Character: Jackson and Jessica from his play
           *a truly marvelous proof

Counting the Days by Cavan Hallman (2011)
  Inspiration song: "All Together Now"
           as performed by Andre 3000
  Character: Yann from his play *Hope*

Little One by Julia Bilbao (2016)
  Inspiration song: "I'll Be Missing You"
           as performed by Puff Daddy
  Character: Trevor from her play *Anniephylaxis*

Hot Air by Katelin Wilcox (2013)
  Inspiration song: "Mr. Tambourine Man"
           as performed by Jack's Mannequin
  Character: Susan from her play *The Magic of Macy's*

If you are interested in reading the source material for any of the inspiration characters, please contact the playwright to request a copy.

Acknowledgments

Thank you to everyone who has contributed to the development of the Very Short Holiday Plays over the first ten years:

Axel Barø Aasen
Lauren Adel
Khairika Al Sinani
Michael Ross Albert
Rachel Alter
Zoe Anastassiou
Christina Baever
Borna Barzin
Mariana Benjamin
Julia Bilbao
Mélisa Breiner-Sanders
Fiona Rae Brunner
John Brunner
Kristina Bylancik
Josh Bywater
Josh Casaubon
Mary Cavett
Annalisa Chamberlin
Nicholas Chan
Greg Cicchino
Lilly Claar
Will Clark
Chris Comfort
Clio Contogenis
Sharon E. Cooper
Matt Cowart
Alison Crane
Tim Creavin
Peter J. Crosby
Jennifer Curfman
Sarah Curtis
Charlotte Cwikowski
Antonia Czinger
Timothy Davis
Erin Deal

Derrick DeMaria
Fernanda Douglas
Sean Drohan
Paul Edwards
Ryan Patrick Ervin
Sara Michelle Evangelista
Jim Fagan
Leah Filley
Kerry Flanagan
Lucy Fleming
Patty Florness
Anne Flowers
Alexandra Fokine
Zoe Frazer
Kathryn Funkhouser
Becky Goldberg
Danny Gorman
Kristin Granade
Gaby Greenwald
Jerzy Gwiazdowski
Cavan Hallman
William Jackson Harper
Bob Hawk
Addie Hays
Kate Moore Heaney
Morgan Hecht
David Higgins
Collins Hilton
Jenan Jacobson
Nathaniel Blake Johnson
Cole Johnston
Dani Joseph
Cindy Kay
Ali Keller
Phil Kenner

Jenny Kirlin
Laura Kiser
Sage Kitchen
Erin Krebs
Helene Kvinlaug
Kelsey Lake
Kitt Lavoie
Madeleine Lawson
Jessica Levin
Sheilagh Lichtenfels
Connor Lounsbury
Alison McLaughlin
Kelly McCready
Eric Miller
Kendra Mittermeyer
Debbie Monk
Kari Morris
Charlie Murray
Rachel Jay Neuman
Amy Nowak
John-Riley O'Handley
Estelle Olivia
Jacob Osborne
Maja Osterman
Sydney Painter
Erica Pappas
Chris Petty
Jane Pfitsch
Amanda Phelan
Aubyn Philabaum

Jake Phillips
Harry Poster
Michael Poyntz
Lonny Price
Matthew Prigge
Lisa Purrone
Deborah Rath
Jennifer Reichert
Will Rogers
Sarah Jane Schostack
Emily Claire Schmitt
Tanvi Shah
Hannah Sikora
Eileen Silvers
Emily Rose Simons
Helene Skogland
Lynn Spector
Chris Stack
Margaret Stanton
Becky Sterling-Rygg
Belle Stockdale
Gerry Tobin
Mike Tranzilli
Zunairis Velazquez
David Vigliano
Molly Way
Kelly Wetherald
Katelin Wilcox
Alexia Zarras
Roseanna Zerambo

About CRY HAVOC

The CRY HAVOC Company, Inc., is a not-for-profit theater company in New York City committed to creating raw, provocative, and humane theater by approaching all plays – both comedy and drama – as conflicts between individuals struggling to do what each desperately believes is right.

Since its founding in 1997, CRY HAVOC has developed more than 900 new plays, musicals, and screenplays through its active Workshop, Lab, and Studio programs. In that time, CRY HAVOC has also brought more than 50 of these projects to the New York stage, including the world premieres of more than 30 new plays.

Projects developed with CRY HAVOC have also been published, made into award-winning films, and produced in major venues in New York, across the United States, and on every continent around the world.

The CRY HAVOC artistic community is comprised of more than 350 actors, writers, directors, and designers at all levels of training and professional advancement – from college students to seasoned Broadway professionals.

CRY HAVOC is committed to developing the next generation of new play developers through its network of educational programming, including its year-round Apprentice Program and its partnerships with universities including New School University College of Performing Arts, NSKI Høyskole (the Norwegian Actors College), the Actors Studio MFA Program at Pace University, Bucknell University, Georgia College, and the Dobbins Conservatory of Theatre & Dance at Southeast Missouri State University.

For more information, visit www.cryhavoccompany.org.

Made in the USA
Coppell, TX
08 November 2019